# Entrepreneurial Happiness

**Reclaim the Free Time, Profit and Fun You Deserve!**

## Dedication

I passionately believe that running your own business can give you the most amazing life, because ultimately you are in control of who you spend your time with, what you spend your time doing and where you spend it. These 3 choices give you the opportunity to craft the life of your dreams. As a result, I would like to dedicate this to all the young entrepreneurs out there. There has never been a better time to set up your own business, never been a time where you can take on a multinational corporation from your bedroom until now!

As a result, I would like to dedicate this book to the young entrepreneurs of this world. You can do this, and you can create an amazing life for yourself.

In addition to that, I'd like to specifically mention a few people:

Ffion and Bronwyn: I hope one day I can help you set up your own businesses doing whatever it is you have a passion for. Thank you for your understanding that I am not perfect at any of this.

Caryl: I hope some of what is in here can help you make an amazing success of your art. It is incredible. Thank you for your support in everything I do.

Mum & Dad: Thank you for your support over the years. Particularly those words of encouragement that "Trying a career in financial services is a bit like turning pro at golf. If you don't give it a go, you'll never know." It certainly worked and I'm now applying that lesson to some even more exciting avenues!

My Teams: In all of my businesses, and whatever role you play, you guys rock. You continue to strive to better yourselves, our businesses and how we help our clients. Without you guys this couldn't happen.

To all the people who have taken time to write courses and books that I have been able to learn from. Specific thanks to The Strategic Coach® Program, David Batchelor my coach, Andy Harrington, George Kinder & Tony Robbins.

Finally, to all those who read and implement the ideas in this book and go on to create amazing businesses. There is no better reward for a teacher than for his students to surpass his achievements. If I can ever do anything to help you on this journey, please drop me a line at **charlie@thetrusted.team** . I'd love to help.

# Foreword

Through coaching people to grow their visibility, credibility and authority, I get to meet a lot of business owners and entrepreneurs, and, when I chat to them, I see the same concerns time and again. With few exceptions, most are struggling to generate enough leads for their business and ultimately enough profit. They are working too many hours and don't have the work life balance they want. And finally, rather sadly, many of them are falling out of love with their business, and they no longer enjoy what they spend most of their time doing.

If you don't generate enough leads, you don't generate enough income for your business. This massively restricts what choices you can make for your business and your life. It restricts how you market yourself, how many people you employ, and also how much you pay yourself. I dare say you didn't get into your running your own business or being a partner in a bigger business in order to settle for an average life and lifestyle. You did it to create something more special for you and the people around you.

If you get your work life balance wrong, which let's face it, we've all done at times, this can be even worse than not making enough money. You stop doing the things that keep you fit and healthy, and that leads to a downward spiral. Whilst you may not see the signs immediately, the effect on your long-term health can be huge.

Of course, it isn't just you that suffers. When you are working too many hours, you miss out on spending time with the people you care most about. Whether it's your special person, your children growing up, or even your grandchildren, you only get one shot at this life, and once your time has gone, it has gone. Research shows that at the end of their life, people don't regret not working enough hours, or even making enough money; their regrets are centred around the experiences they didn't get to enjoy, and the time they didn't get to spend with people.

Finally, when you run your own business, it is so easy to get bogged down in the elements of the business you think you should do; the elements of your day to day that you have got around to or have no one to delegate to. We all know it is easier to get the job done ourselves than teach someone else to do it; and then there is the worry of whether they'll do it as well as we do it. As a result, I see many business owners dreading more and more of their life in business. They fall out of love with the work they originally had such passion to deliver. The reason I wrote 'Passion into Profit' is because people generally have a huge drive for change at the start of their business, but over time, if they don't become to go to person for their industry the business can fade away.

Over the years I have come to know Charlie extremely well. He initially met me when we were both speaking at The National Achievers Congress, and I am proud to say that I went on to train Charlie on his Public Speaking. He even went on to win an award at our professional speaker's award ceremony that we hold annually. He won that because he is the sort of guy that when he commits to doing something, he makes sure he does it well. He dives right in, quite literally. So much so, that I asked him to speak at my event, Power to Achieve. Since then, he has gone on to speak at his industry's global conference in front of 11,000 of his peers. Like I said, he doesn't do things by halves!

What he achieved with Efficient Portfolio and all of his subsequent businesses, like The Trusted Team, and how they have differentiated themselves from their competition is quite remarkable. Whilst I have very little trust for his peers, I have a huge amount of trust and respect for Charlie. Business isn't just about how much money you make, it's about what you do with it too. Whilst in this book, Charlie doesn't really cover much on that subject, he is one of the few people I would go to, to seek this advice because his business is at the forefront of the industry.

What Charlie has done here in writing Entrepreneurial Happiness, is refine down all of the best ideas he has uncovered on his road to success; he is humble in giving credit to the sources that he has learnt from, but of course it is in the implementation of these ideas that is where the real magic happens. Anyone can read a book: it is what you do with it that counts. What I love about this book is that, if you take its advice, follow its strategies and implement its ideas, you have the ability to make more money, keep more of that money, create better health, wellbeing and relationships, all whilst enjoying life more. What more could you ask for? If you got half as much as that from most books, you'd be delighted.

So, take my advice; read and study this book. The contents are powerful beyond measure. Follow his advice, and you too could create more Entrepreneurial Happiness in your life.

Andy Harrington

Sunday Times Best Selling Author

Passion into Profit – 'How to Make Big Money from Who You Are and What You Know'. To download a free audio copy, please visit **www.efficientportfolio.co.uk/AndyHarrington**

# Prologue

*"How dare you settle for less when the world has made it so easy for you to be remarkable?"* – Seth Godin

Before I sold my Chartered Financial Planning business, Efficient Portfolio, a longstanding client of mine ran a successful carpentry business in the UK, and for the purpose of this book, let's call him Joe. Joe was and still is a lovely genuine gentleman; a real family man who cares deeply for his wife and two children.

Joe worked for a large furniture company in his younger years, but in his forties, he became disillusioned with the way the company treated their customers and their employees, and, like so many people, he saw what was being done wrong and wanted to do it better. He was a good carpenter, very good at design, and he felt that he could create a better product at a better price and give better customer experience.

So, halfway through his working life, Joe decided to a step into the world of entrepreneurship and set up his own business in the form of 'Tables R US'. Just a few years later, they were making amazing furniture, delivering a great customer experience, all at a reasonable price, and their customers really valued what they did. They did a particularly brilliant trade in bespoke kitchens, which is where Joe excelled, because his creativity could really shine through and he could engage with the customer and really get to the heart of what they wanted.

Joe loved what he did, and wanted to make the best of his business, not just for himself, but also for his family too. He worked hard throughout his life, but as he aged he realised that he needed to slow down. He was tired of working long hours and never spending time with his loved ones or pursuing his other passion- golf. With some reluctance, he decided it would be soon time to retire, so Joe wisely started to reengineer Tables R Us so that he could sell the business.

Joe was a forward-thinking guy and he realised he needed help on this, so he sought out the help of a business coach who had been recommended by a friend. With the help of his coach, Joe gradually delegated more of what he did on a daily basis and soon it was finally time to hand over the final piece of the business: the oversite of the new product design. This was the part of his job that Joe loved the most, where he excelled, and the differentiator between him and his competitors; in fact, it was the reason he got into business in the first place.

Joe came to see me at our annual review meeting, where we made sure his financial plan was on track and made changes for the year ahead. Joe's finances were in order, ready for him to retire, and an offer was on the table, to sell Tables R Us. We had built Joe a Lifetime Cash-Flow Forecast, a tool we used to help our clients visualise what their financial future would look like, so he knew that the offer far exceeded the figure he needed to comfortably retire. If he accepted, he would be financially free for the rest of his life, even if he lived to 100, and that was a great feeling for him. Theoretically, he could now accept the offer and retire happily, sailing off into the sunset. But what Joe said to me next was both shocking and inspiring.

With a tear in his eye, Joe said, "Two years ago I was desperate to get out of the business. When I was overworking to keep the business moving forward I really wasn't enjoying it. There was a never-ending list of jobs to do, no time to enjoy what I wanted to be doing outside of work, and no future prospect of that changing. Yes, I loved the products design, but as the business grew, I was getting to do that less and less, and I was getting bogged down with the other stuff. The regulations and legislation around our business was where I was needed most, but I hated it.

"So, I should be really excited about now selling up and retiring, but the problem is, having paid a business coach to help me delegate all of the elements that got me down, recently I've only been doing the parts of the business that I love."

Then came the sucker punch: "So now I only do the parts I love, I don't know that I want to sell or retire! All I do now is design the products, which I adore. Thanks to the team we've built, I can now work on my terms, as little or often as I want. I can engage with the customers, help them with my wealth of experience, and help them get the furniture and kitchen of their dreams, and I love that, so why would I now sell up? I have fallen back in love with my business and my passion! I think I've found the perfect compromise: I can retire, whilst still keeping one hand in the business, so, I think I am going to carry on instead!"

This was fantastic for Joe. He could now sail gradually into retirement working as he wanted, and he only had to do the bits he loved, and he was best at, and he had freed up enough time for his other passions- golf and his family. And do you know what happened? Not only did he enjoy life more, but his business actually increased in profitability. He was working less, loving life more and making more money. Isn't that what everyone is looking for?

This might sound odd, but instead of being elated for Joe I was slightly disappointed for him. He had been running 'Tables R Us' for the last 30 years, and only in the final stage of his working life did he figure out how to have the balance he wanted. Whilst the money wasn't the motivational factor for him, he was now making the kind of income his expertise deserved. Imagine what Joe's life might have been like had he implemented those changes some 20+ years ago? How much more money would he have made? How much more time could he have spent with his young family? And how much more could he have enjoyed those years? And how much lower would his handicap be?

I thought back to my first meeting with Joe. I asked him a searching question I asked everyone at our initial meeting. "Imagine you go to see your doctor, and he shocks you with the news that you only have one day left to live. Ask yourself, what would you be thinking about in that 24 hours?" I distinctly remember that one of Joe's regrets was not spending enough time with his children when they were growing up because he had been working so hard. Whilst he was spending his time creating, putting everything into his business, he had missed his children growing up.

As a dad myself, it is always saddening to hear that someone has lost that time, because they will never get it back. Kids grow up at an alarming rate and that time is precious. Sadly, for Joe, he didn't have to sacrifice as much time as he did; he could have achieved everything so much more easily, effectively, and been better rewarded if he'd acted sooner.

Had Joe employed the methodology of the business coach many years earlier he could have seen even more success in his business, whilst having spent more time with his children as they grew up. Not only that, he would have enjoyed his work so much more.

Hindsight is a wonderful thing, but there is little to be gained by it. I believe in looking forward, not backwards. Really all that we can do is change things for the better now, and that is what this book is about.

# Chapter 1: How Can This Book Help?

*"I'm starting with the man in the mirror."* Michael Jackson.

Would you like your business to be making more money than you know what to do with? What if it was making so much that you are more worried about what you are going to do with it all, rather than where you will make the next breakthrough?

And how would you like to run a business where you only do the things that you love? The time you spend working in the business can be as much as little as you want, so that you relish your time at work, but also have all the free time you need.

If the answer is 'yes' to either or both of these questions, congratulations on taking the first step in creating that compelling new future, because that is the aim of this book.

Do you sit and wonder why you are working harder than you did when you were employed? You may remember thinking that, "if only I ran my own business, I could play more golf, cycle more, travel with my family more and get back into shape", but in reality, you actually have less time now than you ever did! I have no doubt that one of the reasons you liked the idea of setting up your own business was so that you could control your most precious commodity, 'time'. Whether you were previously employed or not, do you get the time for yourself and your loved ones that you need or deserve? It's not so many years ago since I was in this same situation: No time to look after myself to do the things I enjoyed, or to spend time with the people I love most, and it was getting me down. I was successful financially, but what was the point if I couldn't live the life I wanted?

Time is without doubt our most precious commodity. Bruce Lee said, "If you love life, don't waste time, for time is what life is made up of." No amount of money or power can buy you more time.

Have you noticed that time just seems to keep getting faster and faster? There is good reason for this: each year of our life is a smaller percentage of our total life than the previous year, so every year of your life will feel quicker than the last. A scary thought, isn't it? If you want to make changes in your life, you'd better get started now, as there is no time to waste. After all, every hour you waste is another hour you will never get back.

Perhaps you're also frustrated that you never seem to make quite as much money as you think your efforts deserve. You are the bottle neck to the company making more money, and you have hit a ceiling that you just don't seem to be able to breakthrough. Maybe your business is going backwards? Or are you trying to compete in the modern world of technology and innovation, but never really making progress? Or maybe you're just prolonging the inevitable?

Have you ever woken up on a Monday morning with a certain amount of dread? Maybe you were thinking about the endless, monotonous list of crucial but hated tasks? That long list of jobs that you don't enjoy, but if you don't do them will be overlooked. Has the fun drained out of running your own business because you spend too little of your time there pursuing or practising your passion?

Instead, are you faced with the bottomless quagmire of 'admin', such as clearing out your inbox or the in-tray?

If this life of insufficient time, money and enjoyment is where you are at the moment, where would you like to be?

I'd like you to imagine that you now have more money in your business bank account than you are sure what to do with. Money to invest into new projects and ideas; money to reward your team, with what they really deserve, and money to create a business environment that you can all enjoy.  Your money is not just in the business account though, because you have a sizeable personal portfolio that means that you are financially free of the business, and you could stop working at any time, if you chose. The great thing is, that you don't actually want to, because work is now on your terms. Does that sound like a nice predicament?

Imagine that you only work at the elements of the business where you excel, and you absolutely love. The aspect of the business that exemplifies why you set up in the first place; the element that, if it was the only thing you did, you would never 'work' a day in your life. Imagine focusing all your time and energy on that part of the business, with no 'admin'! Wouldn't that be amazing?

And that's not the end of it- imagine you also do it on your terms. You only work the number of hours a week, month or year that you want to. You have all the time you need to explore the world with your loved ones, keep fit and healthy and enjoy the other activities you are passionate about. You are in the best shape of your life, travelling to the best places you've ever seen, and creating the best memories with the people around you. Does that sound like an incredibly rewarding life? It certainly excites me.

If what you're doing now is generating little money, creating hassle and devouring your time, wouldn't you agree that you might need a different approach?

That is why I decided to write this book. Since setting up my first business in 2006, I have attended a multitude of courses, worked with world renowned coaches, and have studied a plethora of books on business and personal development. I was never a keen learner at school, and in fact I really struggled in that environment with all but sport.

When she was 14, I discovered that my eldest daughter, Ffion, suffered with Dyslexia. After taking her through various tests, I became certain that she sadly gets it from me. All of the characteristics that signify Ffion's dyslexia were prevalent in me as a child, so I was never an academic kid. But I did find ways around these battles, and I believe that has helped me in businesses. Research shows that Dyslexia can even be an advantage when it comes to running your own business, because by this stage you are used to finding how to work around problems, and that equips you remarkably well as an entrepreneur.

As an adult, I have developed a passion to make all of my businesses the best they can be, make me the best I can be, and have a whole lot of fun along the way. I have learned a lot, some of which now seems forehead-slappingly obvious, and yet I needed someone else to tell before I actually did anything about it, maybe because you need to hear the message at the right time. I hope the messages in this book land at the right time for you. That is one of the reasons I encourage you to revisit this book again and again. The concepts and exercises in this book are not a one off, to be done and never seen again. Every time you revisit them, you'll do so with a new set of eyes, and a subconscious mind that is trying to solve your most pressing business problems, so every time you visit them new answers will present themselves.

Let's face it, this is a really important topic. We only get to live this life once, and, as we've already established, time is slipping away quicker than we think, so we need to get on and do this. Otherwise, we will be one of those people who sits there sadly lamenting the past's possibilities.

I want you to imagine, many years from now, that you are lying on a bed in a crisp white hospital room. Sunlight streams in through the window, and flowers sit on the table next to you. This isn't just any hospital bed though, this is your death bed, and this is your last day on this earth. And on this day, something incredible happens – another you walks through the door. How do they look? Happier or sadder than you? More or less successful than you? More or less healthy than you?

On this day, in that hospital room, you get to meet the person that you could have become. How do you feel? Are you happy that you didn't become that person, or is the opposite true? How awful it would be to meet someone who is far more successful, someone who has had far more fun, and someone who has made significantly more money and impact on the world than you? How would you feel knowing that if you had made different choices you could have had his amazing life instead? Can you think of anything worse than lying on your death bed thinking about what could have been, and what you should have done with your life?

This 'stuff' is really important. Whether you get this right or not shapes your whole life; and not just yours. It shapes the lives of the people that you love the most. It shapes what adventures they will experience, how much quality time they get to spend with you, and the memories they will make. Could there be a more important subject to study? This impacts everything you can account for at the end of your life, so let's spend some time together improving how we go about it.

So why do you need to do this now? Think back to Joe. He missed his children growing up because he didn't make these changes soon enough. You can watch your life go by, and miss your opportunity, or you can get on and do it now.

If your most limited resource is time, then why on earth would you not make these changes in your business now? You could enjoy your time at work more, have the time to create special memories with those important to you, look after yourself better, and maybe even have more money to create the life you love. Can you really afford to wait on areas of your life that are as important as this? If you want to create this amazing new life for yourself, you need to take action now.

\*\*\*

Michael Gerber, the author of the brilliant 'The E-Myth Revisited: Why Most Small Businesses Fail', a must-read book for any business owner, uses the phrase 'working on your business as opposed to working in it.' I love this saying, because it sums up perfectly how we create a successful business that will lead to entrepreneurial happiness. Most small business owners are so busy working in their business, they don't have the time to work on making it better. That impacts their business effectiveness, allows them to continue to make the same mistakes and stops them reaching their potential. That's what this book is about. It is about identifying how you can work smartly '<u>on</u>' your business to make it better.

Within this book I will share the secrets and the tools that helped me achieve success with Efficient Portfolio, and in my other businesses, such as my coaching company, The Trusted Team. I share the techniques that you can use and the questions that you need to answer, but only you will have the answers. You have the answers for your life and business within you, you just need someone to ask you the right questions. **You can win the business race, as long as someone gives you the right track to run on**.

In addition to the tools and techniques, there is a hidden message within this book. You may not get it the first time you read it, so you might need to read it more than once to pick up on this subtler point. When you do you will realise that you have even more power within you than you than you thought. I hope you find it.

I hope this book helps you change your life, and the lives of the people you love most. I read a lot, and where I am able to, I'll give credit to the sources of my wisdom. This won't always be possible though, as sometimes I cannot recall where I got it from, or it's a blended solution from a variety of sources. If I fail to give credit to anyone or anything that has helped me on my journey, I apologise in advance. There are no new ideas, just recycled ones, and this is my attempt to recycle the most valuable ones I have picked up from the books I've read, the courses I've attended, and the people I have spoken to.

One final warning. I am pretty sure I am Dyslexic (*why on earth did they make that word so difficult to spell?*). Don't worry, I am not looking for sympathy. I am blessed with the gift of Dyslexia, and I am sure this has helped me in business. That said, it does mean my spelling and grammar is a little ropey at times. So please forgive me in advance if it does not always meet your expectations. Life is not a game of perfect, and nor shall this book be.

Read it, enjoy it, then action it. A million ideas will change nothing; one purposeful action can change everything!

# Chapter 2: My Story

*"It's in our moments of decision, our destiny is shaped."*
*Tony Robbins.*

You may be wondering, who is Charlie Reading and why should I listen to him? I'd be asking these exact questions, so it's only fair that I give you a bit of background as to where I have come from and how I can help you to achieve time, fun and profit in your business.

Have you ever had a time when you were lost, and didn't know where your future was taking you? If you had been with me on an October evening of the year 1998, you'd have seen me in the kitchen of my parent's 200-year old stone farmhouse that was nestled in the heart of the beautiful Rutland countryside.

On that October evening I was sitting on the huge wooden dresser that was home to Mum's wide array of blue and white crockery. The Aga generated a warmth not needed for that time of year, but ensured the room glowed as the heart of the house. Laying in front of it was Twigg, my short-legged, rough haired Jack Russell, and Kirby, our yellow Labrador, exactly where cade lambs had lain over former winter months.

Sitting on the dresser, I said, "Dad, I have had it with farming. It's only been 4 months since I finished my degree at Newcastle, and I am already being driven crazy by agriculture. I know I have helped you on the farm since I was 15, but that was always a means to an end. This is different now that I've finished my education, there is no end, and I hate it. I cannot spend the rest of my life sitting on a tractor hour after hour listening to Test Match Special and Atlantic 252. If this is all there is to my life, then I want out."

My Dad, a smaller, balder, slightly less good-looking version of me, said "Charles"- my Dad is one of the only people to call me by my birth name- "Don't farm because I did. It is there for you if you want it, and we can diversify into something that interests you more if you wish, but if you don't want to farm, then you need to find something else you want to do. You need to do some serious thinking, but if you do want to step away from farming, that is ok with me, just as long as you do something worthwhile with your life. You only get one shot after all, and if farming isn't for you, then you need to go and plough your own furrow. If you work hard at whatever you do, I am sure you will be successful. If you don't give it a go, you'll never know whether you could have made it."

It was at this juncture I thought I'd air an idea. "Kate and I have been together now for over a year, and with her dropping out of Uni, I think maybe we should go travelling together. Go see the world, and hopefully that might give me some idea as to what I want to do. I could use the money that Grandad left me in his Will; that should last me around 6 months if I am careful. Kate wants to go to South Africa to see where her Mum grew up, I want to go to New Zealand, Australia and Thailand because of the stories I've heard from John, my old house mate in Newcastle, and maybe that will give me some inspiration."

Fast forward just a few months, and I am sat on the pavement in Perth, Western Australia with Kate. The heat was intense, and so was the atmosphere. We had finished travelling around South Africa, an experience that had expanded my mind. The travelling, the scenery, the culture and my first safari had opened my eyes to a world I had not seen before.

Whilst the travelling had been amazing, our relationship had not. I had found an enthusiasm for exploring the world, culture and nightlife that I had lacked at University, but Kate, younger than me, still wanted to lie in and turn in early. The cracks were starting to show.

A large silver Mercedes pulled up in front of us. A large gentleman in a smart, expensive looking suit, open necked, crisp, white shirt and dark glasses got out of the driver's door. "Charles? Hi I'm Bill. Nice to meet you. I can see the Reading and Marks similarities. It's been a long time since I saw those in the flesh! Welcome to Australia."

Meeting a relative who you'd only heard of just a few months prior seemed like quite a daunting experience. Meeting strangers along the coast of South Africa had seemed a lot less scary, maybe because of the anonymity or their lack of expectation of who I'd turn out to be; but, whatever the reason, spending time with some of the poorest people on the planet, experiencing life through their eyes had felt easy compared to this.

"I want to take you on a tour of Perth before I take you back to mine for dinner" he said, in a distinctly Aussie accent. "It's been 20 plus years since I left Dad's butchery business and emigrated here. Since then, I have created a market leading estate agency business. You see that amazing castle overlooking the sea there, we sold that. You see this incredible mansion overlooking Cotteslowe Beach, we sold that too. Every morning I woke up early, and I park up here.

I swim along Cotteslowe Beach, and then me and a few other successful business owners have breakfast in a cafe called Beaches. I then head into the office."

"Wow." I thought, "what a cool start to the working day!"

At his house that evening, I was awestruck with the eclectic worldwide artefacts that adorned the walls. Carvings from Indonesian, paintings from South East Asia, and loads of indigenous Australian art. I wondered how he'd amassed such an extensive collection. "Charles," he said whilst sipping a large glass of red wine over dinner, "I always take a minimum of 3 months a year off. Generally, I travel around Australia, as there is so much to do here. I love diving, and I love exploring the amazing nature we have, but I also love to travel the world too. I work smart, so I don't have to work hard."

"Work smart so I don't have to work hard", now that is an interesting saying. This was a very different side to running a business than I had seen on the farm, where it was all about working harder than the guy next door. How could it be possible for him to have 3 months off each year, and have more money than he seems to know what to do with? Is that even allowed?

I was inspired. I wanted to be a businessman like my Uncle Bill. I didn't know anything about what he did, but I knew I wanted the independence he had, and to lead the same exciting life. For the first time I realised the benefit of running your own business. It had been under my nose my entire life, but I had not seen it for what it really was. It was an opportunity to craft your own future, but there were different ways you could achieve this, and Uncle Bill seemed to have it pretty good. But how could I possibly do what Uncle Bill had done? He had it all. But I had no idea of what I wanted to do or where to start.

Fast forward to the September of the year 1999. I am in Russell Square House in Central London. It's a huge open plan office, packed full of desks housing nothing but a solitary phone. The office was tired looking, and the smell of burnt coffee and stale cigarette smoke filled the air. This wasn't however a calm office; it was more like a scene from the Wolf of Wall Street. Over 50 men in pin striped suits and white shirts dotted the open-plan floor, phones glued to their ears, with stretched cords tethering them to their respective desks. They strutted in circles, or as far as the phone cords permitted, squawking down the line, like frustrated battery hens.

I followed a huge, imposing bald guy, who had introduced himself as Justin, through the path between the desks. The pinstriped sea was only broken by my green sports jacket, and my rather hideous blotchy tie. Astronauts could have spotted me from space the difference was so marked! Was this really the guy that had placed an advert in the Farmer's Weekly?

Justin sat me down, in a seat half the size of his. He looked down over me and boomed; "There are 2 types of people in this world. 'People A', and 'People B'. 'People A' go and work for a big company. They get to earn a good salary. They give all their hard work for their employer, and when they are old, and if they are lucky, they leave with a carriage clock. Then there are People B'. They usually earn less than their friends to start with. They often have to work harder, to start with. But because 'People B' are self-employed, over time they earn more than 'People A', and as well as that, they control their time, and they build up a business they can sell. Which one are you?"

This is easy I thought. The words of Uncle Bill and Dad ringing in my ears, I confidently said "I am definitely in 'People B'. I want to control my own destiny and to make the money I deserve".

"In that case Charlie, you are in. It's commission only. We'll give you one week of financial advice training, and one week of sales training. After that, we'll get you to call your family, mates, and complete strangers; cold calling if you must, and we'll show you how to sell them pensions and life insurance. You're not independent, you are selling one company's products that aren't even that good, but don't worry about that, because we'll show you how to sell them anyway. You'll struggle like crazy, and 95% of people quit within a couple of months, but if you do make money at it, there might well be a good business in it for you!"

Ok, that isn't what he actually said, but that is probably what he should have said, because that's what it was! Had he said this, I may have still given it a shot though, as this was my chance to do my own thing, although I am not sure my Dad would have been quite as supportive.

So, I fell into Financial Services by mistake, and it turned out I was quite good at it. I found that I loved helping people save for their future, protect their family, and make the most of the money they earned.

What I didn't like was the commission hungry, product pushing, target focused companies that seemed to fill the industry. I had found a job I loved, but an industry I hated, so I constantly tried to find ways to do it better. One thing that was working though was the concept of being self-employed. Reaping what you sow, and directly benefiting from the successes I created sat perfectly with me. I loved that concept and wouldn't have had it any other way. So much so that, whilst trying to find a less commission focused business, I did go for an employed interview. I could not get over the concept of having to be in the office, regardless of whether I had hit my target or not, and there was a mutual agreement that I would not suit being an employee.

But just as the clouds were clearing for my career, I received some devastating news from Australia. My Uncle Bill, the man that had it so right in my eyes, had taken his own life. How could this happen? He had the perfect life, why would he do that? Clearly there must be more to life than just success, but I still wasn't sure what it was!

\*\*\*

It's some years later now, to be specific a Sunday night in April 2011, and I am stood in the Excel Arena in London. I'm stood in a huge room. It's dark, and I am surrounded by 6,000 people. There is an insane tension in the air, because these people are screaming, yelling and crying out in pain and anger. The sounds were as painful as they were deafening, and to make it worse, as someone that very rarely cries, there are tears pouring down my face. I am not in the middle of some national disaster though, I am actually an event called 'Unleash the Power Within', by a guy called Tony Robbins.

Tony Robbins is the world's top life and performance coach. He has taken top sports stars like Andre Agassi back to number 1, has coached several of the world's most successful traders, and has also mentored a number of American Presidents, including Bill Clinton. He charges £1m per day for 1-2-1 coaching, but he is most famous for his transformation events, and this is what I and 5999 other people were attending.

'Unleash the Power Within' is a 4-day event that typically runs from 9 am until gone midnight each day. You may be wondering, how can a seminar last that long? Well, this is no normal seminar; this is more like a rock concert where the music is the sound of people literally rewriting their past and future lives.

'Unleash the Power Within' is most famous for 'The Fire Walk'. This isn't something you build up to over the 4 days but is actually done on the very first night. Caryl, my wife, and I, headed out into the darkness of the London night around 10.30 on that first evening, and down in the car park ahead of us were 35 lanes of burning hot coals, and 6000 people chanting in order to get themselves in the right state so that they don't burn. As your bare feet step out onto the burning hot coals, you have to be sure you are in the right mindset to conquer it, otherwise you will burn. And if you can achieve that, you can achieve anything.

But it wasn't 'The Fire Walk' that changed my life that weekend, it was in amongst the screaming, shouting and crying on the Sunday night that I had an epiphany. Out of the darkness came a booming voice, as formidable as a lion's roar. I say that because Tony is a big guy. Some call him the 'King of the Coaching Jungle'. At 6 feet 7 inches tall, he has hands seemingly bigger than tennis rackets, and teeth bigger than dinner plates. He is an intimidating guy at the best of times, but what he said in that moment, shook me to the core.

With our eyes closed, he asked us: "What decisions have you been making over the last 5 years that have led you to where you are today? What limiting beliefs do you have that are damaging your life today? What will your life look like 5, 10 and even 20 years from now if you carry on making these decisions? Because it's in our moments of decision that our destiny is shaped."

I thought to myself, "5 years ago I decided to set up my own financial planning company, Efficient Portfolio, because I was sick of our industry. That has gone really well from a business point of view, but at what cost? Am I really making a sufficient sum to justify the hours I am putting in? 1 year ago, I set up The Rural Business Community, my serviced office business. That has also been really successful, but I have had to give up huge amounts of my family time. I now have a wife and 2 beautiful daughters, Ffion and Bronwyn, and I am not spending anywhere near enough time with them. I am slogging my guts out to run these businesses successfully, and whilst they are doing well, they could be more profitable.

"And look at yourself Charlie. You are in the worst condition of your life. You must be 3 stone overweight. You're eating the wrong stuff, drinking too much and you've had to give up playing sport because you are too busy. You are an embarrassment."

So, when Tony said to imagine the worst that your life could look like 20 years from now, because of these decisions, that was easy. I could see a sweaty, wrinkly me sat in a grotty 1 bedroom flat. I weighted 20 stone, my gut was hanging over the side of the chair, pizza boxes surrounded me on the floor. Caryl and the girls had left me years before because I was a disgrace, and my businesses had failed because I was in no fit state to run anything. I couldn't do any of the things I loved, because I was in no physical condition to do so, and I couldn't spend time with the people who I loved because they had long since given up on me. This horror of a life was mine, 20 years from now, unless I made some changes now.

Then Tony said something that still plays on repeat in my mind. "If you make the same decisions today as you made yesterday, you'll get the same results tomorrow as you got today." Can you relate to that? What decisions are you making today but expecting a different result from?

I left Unleash the Power Within a level of determination I had never had before. In the years leading up to Tony Robbins' event, I'd participated in various workshops like Dan Sullivan's Strategic Coach®, but I'd only been working on the business, and never anything else. Despite some rest bite during family holidays, my working days were ridiculous, and prohibited me from exercising and spending time with the people I loved. I needed to find ways to work smarter, not harder, just like Uncle Bill had.

I set off with a new purpose, and a determination to learn and grow into the best person I could be. I made some immediate changes to the way I worked, some in line with what I'd learnt in Strategic Coach®, but with a new level of emphasis. I signed up for Tony Robbins' Business Mastery, another 4- day event focusing purely on your business; I attended events like T Harv Ecker's Guerrilla Business Intensive and Enlighted Warrior Training Camp; and I read more than ever. More importantly, Caryl and I redesigned from scratch the way we ate, and also how we scheduled our time to ensure we factored in quality family time and exercise.

Fast forward again to September 2015, and I am sitting in the meeting room of our first Rutland office, with a long-standing client of mine called David. Sat in flat cap, overalls and socks, having left his wellington boots in reception, this aging farmer declared, "Charlie, it's time for me to retire. The time has come for me to step aside from the farm, and thanks to all your help, particularly the Lifetime Cash-Flow Forecasting, I am comfortable that I have all the money that I need for the rest of my life. The problem is, what am I going to do all day? Am I going to be bored hanging around the house? And what about my health, I've always been working on my feet. Have I got to swap my overhauls for Lycra and start attending spinning classes?"

"David this is not the first time I have heard these concerns; in fact, I have heard them many times. That's why I am quite excited to tell you that this morning, a massive box arrived at my office. Inside that box are the first copies of my first book, 'The Dream Retirement: How to Secure Your Money and Retire Happy', and I'd like you to have the first copy. I like you to pay particular attention to the second half of the book, as that is where I focus more on how you spend your time and how you stay fit and healthy."

David was a very special client to me. Not just because he was a long-standing client, but also because he is my Dad and he got the first copy of my book.

The book 'The Dream Retirement' led on to a bit of a roller coaster of success for me and Efficient Portfolio. I started being feature on the radio, on TV and in the newspaper, and at the point I sold it, Efficient Portfolio was known as one of the top financial planning practices in the UK. That's not me blowing my own trumpet- that was what The Sunday Telegraph, The Sunday Times and New Model Adviser all said. We were also a Chartered firm, which put us in the top 14% of all practices in the UK. In the 6 years leading up to its sale, we also increased our new business sales by 50% in 5 of those final 6 years, all whilst taking 3 months off every year.

I am 3 stone lighter since I made that initial encounter with Tony Robbins, and in recent years have completed numerous marathons and I am an ultra-marathon runner. At the time of writing, I am also a 6-time Ironman finisher and have just qualified for the championships in Kona, Hawaii, in 2024.

In addition to my sporting achievements, I have also written four books, and I am working on my fifth, and now get to speak on stages around the world, for example when I was given the opportunity to speak to 1100 peers in Miami Beach.

When The Dream Retirement was first published, I was asked to share the stage with internationally renowned speakers like Andy Harrington and Gerry Robert. I tell you all this not to impress you, just to demonstrate that this is all possible for anyone. I am sure I could take it too far further extremes, but actually I love what I do and currently wouldn't change the balance I have in my life.

There is nothing special about me. All I have done is gone out and found others that have already mastered the elements I want to master and have learned from them. I have read their books, attended their courses, and spent quality mentoring time with them. I am not saying I have it designed perfectly, but I personally feel that I have designed a pretty extraordinary life, and I have no doubt that the next year will be even better than this one.

As it currently stands, I run four companies:

**Accelerate Adviser Solutions**: An outsourcing solution to give financial advisers their time back by taking on administration, plan writing and research, plus helping them to optimize their operations. **www.accelerateteam.co.uk**

**The Trusted Team**: A coaching and networking company that helps entrepreneurs and professionals grow their business whilst working less and enjoying both their work and their personal lives more. **www.thetrusted.team**

**The Hub and Spoke**: A business hub and café with a professional focus in the week and a cycling focus at the weekends. **www.thehubandspoke.co.uk**

**Efficient Portfolio Wealth**: Connecting clients with expert financial planners and providing financial education across a range of topics and needs. **www.efficientportfolio.co.uk**

And do you know what? The less I work, the more money my businesses seem to make. The happier and healthier I am, the better I am at doing what I do best. The more I merge what I describe as fun with business, the more successful we become.

I hope you can see that I have created the perfect blend of profitability, free time and fun in my businesses, and life. You will not achieve the same as I have done solely by reading this book, however, you may achieve the same or even better than me if you read the book and continue to carry on the practices I'll talk you through. To help you continue your journey, throughout this book I'll show you how we might be able to help you in the future.

So, let's get started.

# Chapter 3: Best Friend Forever

*"Losers have goals, winners have systems."* Scott Adams

At the point of writing, I have had around 20 years of experience of being self-employed, and I have discovered that if you are truly going to create Entrepreneurial Happiness, you need to master 3 main areas.

Firstly, you need ensure you are making **Money**. If you aren't doing that then business life is definitely stressful: you cannot afford to pay yourself what you deserve; you cannot afford to enjoy the holidays that allow you to recharge; you cannot afford to invest in new systems, marketing opportunities or new people; and, ultimately, you cannot grow your business. So, it is a given, you need to make money.

A lack of the right number of the right calibre of leads restricts businesses. This leads to poor cash-flow, which is the killer of so many small businesses. Lack of investment can also kill business growth and prohibits it from reaching its potential. In the early stages of business, income generation can also be slow, and life can be very 'hand to mouth', so we need to find ways to make money, and quickly. It would be easier if you had a management team taking care of all of these complicated details, but you don't, so what can you do?

If you want to make more money, you need more leads, more client enquiries and more buy-in, but that is easier said than done. How can you consistently find more of your best fit clients, and make sure that they are desperate to work with you? If you can crack this nut, you can have a far better nourished business, as you have a consistent stream of new money coming in. Again, it is easier said than done though.

Making more money creates more problems. What should you do with it, how do you track it, and how can you see what your business and personal financial future looks like? You need to be able to predict what is coming if you are to keep your company's finances, and your own wealth, growing rather than shrinking.

In order to create Entrepreneurial Happiness, we need to find more robust ways to build, manage and protect our money.

But Entrepreneurial Happiness is about so much more than just the money; you need to be the master of your **time**. Only once you have cracked this, can you work in/on your business on your terms, and enjoy all of the other things that are important to you. Without this, you will be working late, missing your children's sport's days, and not creating memories with the people you love. Without time you may also neglect your health, and to run a healthy business, you need to be a healthy business owner.

But where do you find time? The saying even goes, 'if you want something doing, ask a busy person!' How can that make sense? Do they have more than 24 hours in their day? No, they just have better understood how to manage their time and to get the most out of it. Are you making the most of your time? Could you be achieving so much more with the help of better strategies and tools? What are you missing out on by not having these in place?

It's difficult running your own business. Your clients want your time, but so do your employees. It's often a misconception that your employees won't be able to do the job as well as you can. In reality they are more than capable, but, they can't if so much of what you need them to do is in your head!

Maybe you are also struggling with finding enough time because your business is built around dealing with people on a 1-2-1 basis, and this massively restricts the amount of work you can take on. There are only so many hours in the day, and therefore only so many clients you can deal with.

Finally, if you don't have enough time, and you are spinning too many plates, which one is the one that gets dropped first? Your health? If you get busy, you stop exercising. You also maybe eat less healthy, and perhaps even drink a little more to destress. An unhealthy business owner leads to an unhealthy business too. A lack of energy, self-discipline and longevity can't be good for any business, and there is only so long coffee and energy drinks will keep you bouncing back.

If you want to create Entrepreneurial Happiness, you need to master making **money** and controlling your **time**, but there is one last piece of the jigsaw to be truly happy: If you want to create true Entrepreneurial Happiness, you need to create **fun** in your business life. Without fun in your business, every day seems like a chore.

It's so easy start to feel unfulfilled if you think you are not moving forward in your life, or not getting better as a person. Jim Rohn said, 'Income seldom exceeds personal development'. In fact, it's one of our 6 human needs, and you won't feel truly happy without it, but more on that later in the book. And it's not just about growing as a person, but as a business too. If you are not going forward, you are going backwards. If you are not continually innovating, then you will be overtaken by your competition, and at a pace where it will be too late to adapt. Your business will have gone in a flash.

Did you know that most of the astronauts who walked on the moon suffered from depression afterwards? Why would that be, when they had achieved their lifelong goals? Shouldn't they be overjoyed? Sadly, achieving their goals was the reason they became depressed. Once you have fulfilled a massive goal, there is nothing to compel you forward, no new purpose to live, and this leads to serious unhappiness. You need a compelling future to pull you forwards, and without one business life will become pretty depressing.

One of the best ways to scale your business is to employ others, but that can feel like a chore in itself. You train your employees to where you need them to be, and then they leave! They don't believe in the business like you do, and don't share your vision. After all, it's just their job, not their life like it is for you.

There are so many aspects that can drag the **fun** out of your business life. As the saying goes, 'if you do a job you love, you'll never work a day in your life'; however, does that still apply when you spend most of your time doing stuff you hate? You need to create **fun** in your business so that you live out your passion every day. Work should be more fun!

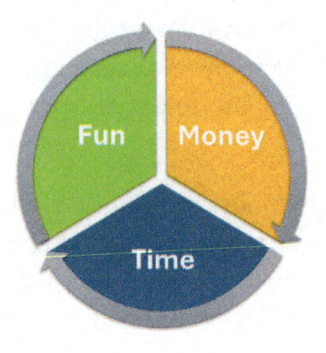

Over my years of experience, reading many books, attending many courses and trying to pick the brains of those I admire and have met, I have discovered that there are a number of key areas that you need to focus on in order to create success in each of these areas.

In order to make this more memorable and easier to explain, I have taken the time to build these into systems, so that hopefully they make more sense. **The Better Future Framework** is a system that I believe has the power to transform your business and personal life forever. It's components certainly have for me.

**The Better Future Framework** is made of 3 key systems, and it is at the backbone of the coaching I provide through The Trusted Team.

### More Money

In order to help you make your business more profitable, and generate more money, I have created **The Profitable**

**Business P.L.A.N**. If you learn and follow the 4 key steps here, you will have the tools to be able to attract more new customers into your business, to ensure that you can make more money. Often the biggest constraint to increasing profits is finding enough of the right customers, so I want to show you how you can find a lot more.

**The Profitable Business P.L.A.N**. will show you how to know exactly what is going on in the business at any one time, so that you understand exactly which elements are working well for you and which need more attention. An early warning system, if you like, to help you avoid running out of cash or customers; it's also the tool that ensure you hit the targets you set yourself.

**The Profitable Business P.L.A.N**. will also show you how to protect your business in case the unexpected happens. We can all plan for a predictable future, but you need to ensure that when the expected comes along, that's it doesn't derail your plan. And it will show how you can maximise the money you make, keeping as much away from the tax man as legally and ethically possible and protecting the money you make in case your business suffers a change of fate in the future. This system will equip you with the tools to help make sure you generate more money and make the most of it when you do.

The concepts inside **The Profitable Business P.L.A.N** allowed me to grow my new business level by a whopping 50% in 5 of the last 6 years at Efficient Portfolio. They also allowed us to increase our new enquiries by a multiple of 7 in just 4 years. They also gave me much greater insight into what is going well and what isn't in all of my businesses, so that I can anticipate problems on the road ahead. They have also allowed me to de-risk my businesses, so that if something unexpected happens, there is less risk of it going under.

**The Profitable Business P.L.A.N** helps you to make more money, more effectively, and with more predictability than ever before.

### More Time

In order to help you take control of your time, I have created **The Free Life Business M.O.D.E.L.**, a 5-step system that will show you how you can scale your business with decreasing input from you, so that you can take more time away. It will show you how you can streamline and delegate, so that you only concentrate on the elements of the business where you excel.

**The Free Life Business M.O.D.E.L** shows you how you can maximise the impact of what you do, so that you can achieve more in less time. It will give you the systems that will allow you to get the most done possible in your time, and make sure you have the time to do all the other important things you cannot currently do. Finally, **The Free Life Business M.O.D.E.L** will show you how to improve your health and wellbeing once you have more free time.

**The Free Life Business M.O.D.E.L** has allowed me to take more and more time out of the business whilst simultaneously running it more effectively, and it making more profit than ever before. Each year I take around 12 weeks of holiday, I rarely work evenings or weekends, and I do not work on Friday afternoons.

In reality I could take more time out if I wanted to, but actually I now enjoy the balance I have. This balance has also allowed me to get into the best shape of my life. As an example, in 2017 I completed a ½ Ironman distance triathlon for the first time. That is 1900m swim - 85km bike - 21km run, something I could not have done before. Now, in 2024, I take part in roughly 2-3 full distance Ironman competitions each year.

Building up to this has taken a lot of training time, but it was the lifestyle that I created that has allowed me to get into a position to be able to do that. Yet, despite me spending less time in my office, my businesses are helping more people and making more money than ever before, and it is thanks to the tools and strategies that I have rolled into **The Free Life Business M.O.D.E.L.**

### More Fun

In order to help you enjoy your business life more, I have created **The E.P.I.C. Business Blueprint**. This 4-step system will help you ensure you become the best possible version of yourself. It will give you, what I believe, is the best way to set and consistently hit clear and exciting goals.

**The E.P.I.C. Business Blueprint** will give you the tools to build an incredible team around you who you love working with, and who live and breathe your vision for the business. It also helps you identify other firms that you can partner with, so that you can both achieve your goals more quickly.

**The E.P.I.C. Business Blueprint** allowed Efficient Portfolio to become one of the best financial planning businesses in the UK. It's also enabling The Trusted Team to flourish and innovate, and it's what we teach our members so they can do the same. The tools, strategies and systems are the reason behind our continued and strong business growth; however, one element alone was the main factor behind what allowed us to increase our business at Efficient Portfolio by 50% in the first year we tried it. It is incredible.

At the same time as my companies getting better and better, I have personally grown a phenomenal amount as a result of the content in **The E.P.I.C. Business Blueprint.** I am a very different person to who I was nearly 20 years ago. A far more focused, determined, organised and efficient version of who set up their first company in 2006.

Without question, I have the best teams working with me that I have ever had. They are far better at their own areas of expertise than I am, and we gel brilliantly, partly because we all buy into the same purpose. They allow me to do what I do best and take care of all of the other aspects of the business, which means I love what I do.

I am a very goal focused person, but I also need to have a clear purpose in everything I do. Thanks to **The E.P.I.C. Business Blueprint,** there is always a more compelling future for me to strive towards. It is this system that shelters me from a world of negativity and keeps me feeling positive about the future, enables me to innovate, enjoy my life and develop a culture of constant and never-ending improvement.

As you can probably tell, I love my life, and I want to share with you the secrets to how I got there, so that you can too.

**Fun** — The E.P.I.C Business Blueprint

**Money** — The Profitable Business P.L.A.N

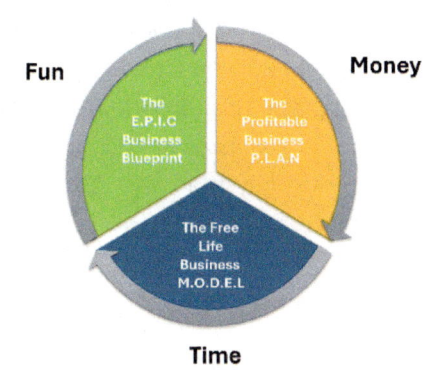

**Time** — The Free Life Business M.O.D.E.L

In a nutshell, if you grasp the concepts within the Better Future Framework, you will be well on your way to finding Entrepreneurial Happiness. That magic balance of making enough money to live the life you want, having sufficient free time to do the things you love, and thriving and having fun at work.

## Chapter Summary

- If you don't learn how to find more customers and ultimately make more money from the work you do, you will be deprived of living the life you deserve.
- If you don't learn how to improve your time management, then you will miss out on living a long and healthy life with the people you care about most.

- If you don't learn how to create fun in your work life, you will end up spending the majority of your life doing something you don't actually enjoy.
- The easiest way to create more money, free time and fun in your business is to follow a proven system. That system is **'The Better Future Framework'**, also known as BFF, because if you follow its principals, it will be your best friend forever!

# Section 1: The Profitable Business P.L.A.N.

The 4-step guide to making more MONEY in your business.

**P**  Partnerships

**L**  Leads

**A**  Amass

**N**  Numbers

# Chapter 4: 'Leads' Lead to More Money

*"Our job is to connect to people, to interact with them in a way that leaves them better than we found them, more able to get where they'd like to go."* Seth Godin

"BREMONT IS AN AWARD-WINNING BRITISH COMPANY PRODUCING BEAUTIFULLY ENGINEERED CHRONOMETERS AT OUR HEADQUARTERS IN HENLEY ON THAMES, ENGLAND."

That's what Bremont's website says. It continues with:

"Life for Nick & Giles English changed significantly one clear day in March 1995. Nick was practicing for an air display with their father Euan. But the 1942 WWII Harvard aircraft they were flying was involved in an accident. Giles, waiting to take off for the next sortie was told that his father had been killed. His brother had broken over 30 bones and probably wouldn't make it.

"Six months later, however, Nick was back in the air and being flown by Giles. But things would never be the same again. Life was too short to waste. The two brothers decided to pursue what they enjoyed most: a life crafting beautifully engineered mechanical devices.

"When they weren't flying old aircraft, Nick & Giles had spent most of their childhood making things in the workshop of their gifted father - an ex-RAF pilot with a PHD in Aeronautical Engineering. Models. Restored cars. They even helped him to build an aircraft they still fly to this day. Euan was also passionate about mechanical timepieces. He would often bring home an old clock from an auction for the brothers to try and get going again. The passion lives on in the classic curve of a Bremont timepiece."

An incredibly moving story, but what's this got to do with making more money? Simon Sinek, in his brilliant book 'Start with Why', highlighted the merit of beginning everything client facing with why you do what you do. Whether it is your marketing, your recruitment, or improving your teamwork, one of the most powerful aspects to promoting and improving your business is to ensure everyone, including yourself, knows why you do what you do. And this is what Bremont have done.

Bremont are probably the most successful non-Swiss company in the high-end watch sector. They have had huge success since launching, and a large reason behind that is their story. And not just their initial story; every watch has its very own story. For example, the Bremont MB1 was only sold to people who had ejected out of a plane using a Martin Baker ejector seat. Niche market or what! That watch has sold second hand on eBay for $120,000, so they have certainly created demand. But why are people willing to spend this sort of money on a watch? Because it looks nice, or because of the story behind it?

How can you build the same hype and success around your brand or service? The first step, of course, is that you need to know your own story. Why do you do what you do? I told mine in Chapter 2, but I also use it whenever I talk to a new audience. If you'd like to see me telling my story, the best example can be found in my free virtual workshop called '3 Steps to Entrepreneurial Happiness', which you can access here: **www.thetrusted.team/virtual-workshops**

To help you find your why, I have put together an exercise. This can be found in The Entrepreneurial Happiness Workbook, that you can download for free from **www.thetrusted.team/books/entrepreneurial-happiness/**

We once ran a recruitment campaign for a new team member at Efficient Portfolio. Let's just say that we were underwhelmed by the response, so something needed to change. We ran the same advert again just a week later, but this time we added our 'why statement' of 'Creating a better future through inspirational Financial Planning'. The remainder of the advert was identical, but our responses quadrupled and all because we 'Started with Why!'

If you want to boost the effectiveness of every piece of marketing you do, you always need to think back to 'Start with Why', because people buy into why you are doing what you do, and, as a result, they buy into you as a business and as an individual much more. I would recommend that you write a single sentence, like the one that we used in our advert and use it at any available opportunity.

Once you've got this succinct why statement, I would then suggest that you build a paragraph about your why and, ideally, a full story too. I save mine in an ever-growing file called 'The Marketing Bible', where I archive everything I do that involves marketing. This means that I have a consistent source for marketing copy, and I can make one piece of content serve me multiple times. We'll add more to The Marketing Bible later on but, for now, make sure you at least have one sentence on your why!

## Reading Minds

*"If you think education is expensive, try ignorance!"* Derek Bok

I am a big believer in setting goals, because I achieve so much more as a result. After I employed my first team member, I decided I needed help in the way I was going to grow and manage my business. I had heard about a workshop for entrepreneurs called The Strategic Coach® Program through some of the top people in the financial services sector and decided that if I was going to get close to what they were doing, I needed to learn the same tools and strategies.

The Strategic Coach® Program seemed like a huge commitment and cost at the time, but I knew if I was going to be successful, I needed to hang on and learn from the best our industry had to offer. The programme, founded by Dan Sullivan, is a quarterly workshop where a group of entrepreneurs meet to learn new strategies on how they can improve the way they run their lives and their businesses.

There was a minimum earning level to be able to join the programme and I remember when I first saw Dan speak, I was below that level. I decided that when I was above it, I could afford to employ someone to help me and, at that point, I would need help creating a better business that was no longer just in my head. A couple of years later I made what felt like a huge leap of faith. Particularly where learning is involved, it can feel so expensive, and you question whether it will pay for itself, let alone deliver everything it promises.

What I loved about Strategic Coach® was that it forced you to spend 1 day a quarter working on the business, as opposed to working within it. It was an amazing opportunity to be a small fish in a big pond, and when I was bouncing ideas off people about changes I needed to make in my business, it was usually with people who had long since made those changes themselves. This programme is not industry specific, it works for all business owners, but I do think it works particularly well for people in professional practice.  You could say that it was one of the inspirations for my own coaching business, which I founded several years later.

One of the things that Dan Sullivan is most famous for is his 'R-Factor Question®' [1]. As a result, before we go any further, I would like to ask you my version; it isn't quite the same as Dan's, but it will achieve the same result:

*If we were sat here 1 year from now, what must have happened for you to be happy with the progress you have made? What concerns have you got that you'd like to overcome, and what opportunities have you got that you would like to maximise.*

Take some time to answer this question and write down your answers.

What you should now have are some clear goals that you need to achieve over the next year. You should have identified some concerns in both your work and personal life that you need to resolve, and some opportunities that

---

[1] Please visit **www.StrategicCoach.com** to learn more about the Strategic Coach® Program and/or the R-Factor Question®

you need to have maximised in that time too. If you do not write down your goals regularly already, make this a new habit. I'll come back to this later and give you my own amazing system that will ensure that you hit these goals, but the first step to achieving anything is to firstly define where you need to be.

At Harvard University, a study was conducted to see what percentage of graduates documented their goals: The results showed that only 3% of graduates did this. Probably not that surprising, you may say, but the percentages were not the most interesting part of the study. It transpired that the 3% who had been regularly writing down their goals were worth more than the 97% combined.

Still not convinced? Well, think of writing down goals like a game of bowling. If I asked you to get a strike, knocking all 10 pins down with one ball, while you were looking at and aiming at the pins, you'd have a fighting chance. You'd probably not get a strike every time but hopefully almost every attempt would take out some pins. But what if I asked you to try whilst wearing a blindfold? You've just seriously hampered your chances of scoring a strike, and maybe even bowling in the right lane!

The message here is simple: if you can't see where you're going, you have very little chance of reaching your destination. Writing down your goals is a good way to plot out your route, especially when used in conjunction with my system. If we're sticking with the bowling metaphor, the system I've created has the same effect as using the ball barriers that stop the ball dropping into the gutter. More on that later though.

For now, I want you to focus on the fact that you have identified some 'worries' that you want to eliminate over the next year, and some 'opportunities' that you want to maximise. I would imagine that if you achieve all of them, that would mean this year has been a good year. If that isn't the case, go back and rethink on a bigger scale! What would make you truly proud of what you'd achieved?

Your goals are not the only ones to consider. To illustrate my point, I'm going to sell you a widget. This widget is called The Future Transformer. My Future Transformer widget is guaranteed to deliver all the items you listed above. Whatever you want, the Future Transformer is GUARANTEED to deliver it. My question is, would you like to buy my Future Transformer widget? Of course you do! It guarantees to deliver the most important things over the next year. The question is, how much would you be willing to pay? £1000? £100,000? £1m? I suppose it depends on the size of your dreams!

This is evidently a fictional product, but if I did have a 'magical widget' that promised to deliver you the most important things over the next 12 months, the chances are you'd buy it. So, would it not make logical sense to know the answer to the former question for your own customers and clients? Wouldn't it be much easier to sell your product or service to that new customer or client if you understood what their most important goals were for the year ahead, so that you could show them how your product or service could help get them there?

Let me give you an example. A few years ago, I read 'Leading' by Sir Alex Ferguson and Michael Moritz. In it, Sir Alex tells the story of him trying to sign Paul 'Gazza'

Gascoigne for Manchester United. Playing for his hometown club, Newcastle United, at the time, Gazza was the young rising star in English football, and Sir Alex wanted him at Manchester United. So, he went into his meeting with Gazza with a well-oiled and polished sales-pitch to win him over.

Sir Alex's opening gambit was to build some rapport with Gazza: firstly he regaled him with the success stories of fellow Geordies who had played for Manchester United; he then told Gazza that he would be walking in the steps of his hero, Bobby Charlton; and finally he focused on the wonderful history of the top players at Manchester United who went on to become the top players for England. Well versed at signing the players he wanted, Sir Alex was confident that these tales would get him his man.

But do you remember Gazza going on to become a star at Manchester United? Of course you don't, because Gazza never took up Sir Alex's deal. Instead of being lured by Sir Alex, Gazza signed for Tottenham Hotspur instead. What could Spurs have offered him that Sir Alex couldn't? It turns out it was a house in Gateshead for his mum! Had Sir Alex Ferguson asked what was most important to Gazza before he went steamrolling into his pitch, do you think that Gazza may have signed for Sir Alex instead? Given the size of the club at the time, I reckon if a house in Gateshead was what Gazza wanted, that's what he would have got, and perhaps his and England's footballing history would have been very different.

Whether you're sending out marketing letters or you are face-to-face with a client in a sales meeting, you need to make your content meaningful to that person. Furthermore, it's all very well generating more leads with your marketing strategy, but if you want to convert more of those leads, you need to be able to help your clients in the most impactful way possible. If you want to truly show your clients how your product or service can help them deliver their most important goals, you first need to ask what they are! Ask all of your potential clients this question and the insights you will get will help you transform your business into the one of your client's dreams.

Furthermore, over time you will notice patterns and common goals amongst your best fit clients. This will allow you to tailor everything you do towards these. That means that when you do your marketing, you will already be appealing to your best fit client's core goals, without even knowing it for sure yet. By doing this, your marketing just became a whole lot more powerful, and generates more leads.

At the Trusted Team, we use a tool called 'The Ideal Client SWOT' to help with this, which helps you to identify the strengths, weaknesses, opportunities, and threats to your clients, and allows you to come up with solutions to help them. If you'd like to see a real-life example of this tool, please just drop us an email to **hello@thetrusted.team**

Be meaningful, be personal, get more leads and help more people.

## Referrals Are the Key
If you want to receive, first you must give. That is the rule, not just of business, but of life too.

One of the best examples I have seen of this principle was from Dropbox when they first launched. Every user who signed up was encouraged to refer a friend. In return for doing so, they were given a huge amount of free storage, simply by providing an email address. This quick, painless act saw Dropbox catapult themselves to success very early on and become an exceptionally lucrative business.

In his monumental book 'Influence', Dr Robert Cialdini talks about how a university professor sent Christmas cards to a group of complete strangers. He received replies from a good number of these people. They had never heard of or met this professor but, having received a card, they felt compelled to send one in reply. When someone does something for us, we feel compelled to return the gesture.

In the same book, Dr Cialdini goes on to tell a story of Ethiopia and Mexico, and a $5000 relief aid payment. In 1985 Ethiopia was in the heart of devastating poverty. Its food supply had been ravished, its economy in ruins and its people suffering as a result of an unrelenting drought and disease. To hear of a relief payment of $5000 sent from Mexico to Ethiopia should not sound that unexcepted. However, that relief payment didn't go from Mexico to Ethiopia; it actually went from Ethiopia to Mexico. The money had been sent to help out with the devastation caused by an earthquake in Mexico City.

To understand this better, we need to look back to 1935, when Mexico had sent aid to Ethiopia when it was invaded by Italy. Despite the incredible need for the money in their homeland of the drought-stricken Ethiopia, the need to reciprocate and pay back the debt had remained for a half century.

The power of reciprocity seems to know no bounds , so if you want to receive more referrals, you first need to think about how you can give. How can you create so much value and good feeling that the recipients of your gift are delighted to work with you?

If you want to find more clients, there is a huge resource that can help you: your existing clients! By their very nature, your clients have already bought into what you do. They want to see you do well and they want to help you do that, because that makes sure that you are there to continue helping them in the future. So, why is it that some businesses get loads of referrals and others none?

The answer boils down to how businesses deal with the following questions:

1. How often do you make your clients think about referring someone to you?
2. How easy do you make it to refer someone?
3. How do clients benefit when they do refer someone?
4. How does the referral benefit the person being referred?

Nobody wants to be pestered with being asked for referrals. Even worse, nobody wants to feel like they are pestering people for referrals! When I first joined the dark, sales-driven world of financial services, at the end of the second meeting with a client I was told to ask the newly signed up client for some referrals. I was told to say that it is how we keep their costs down, because it saved on marketing. I would sit there and write the numbers 1 through to 6 on a blank piece of paper, and then go silent. The awkwardness for both of us was horrid.

The clients didn't want to feel pressured into giving referrals, and I didn't want to pressure them, yet it happened across every desk in the office, because that was what we were told we had to do. I still cringe thinking back to those moments. No one wants to be on either side of that conversation, so how can you get more referrals without having those awkward encounters?

Overtime, I have learnt to ask more gently, more often, and to build a process around it. About 4 years before I sold Efficient Portfolio, we got 40 referrals from our clients. That may not sound like a lot for your business, but I can only put it into context by telling you about the year before when we received 21 client referrals. 40 is nearly double the previous year. The year before that it was 8. Again, we doubled the referrals we were getting. The question is how did we manage to achieve that?

One of the ways was by hosting our annual Referral Dinner. This is a meal to thank anyone who has referred us to a new client. It was usually at a Michelin Star restaurant and was a lovely evening. The purpose was to thank those who are keen referees, and to share some quality time and a great experience with them. Of course, this incentive was not something to keep quiet about.

What reward is appropriate is for you to decide. A client was of high value to us, so a Michelin-star dinner was right for our business. I know of one company that takes referred clients on a cruise for a couple of days! If a client's worth justifies the cost then go for it! Personally, I would shy away from giving money, especially if regulation dictates you can't, but a voucher or some flowers could be a cost effective and ethical solution. Ideally though, make it an interactive experience, and a dinner works well.

But what about the client who has been referred? We used to give any referrals into our business a free Exploration Meeting with one of our advisers, worth £197. If you can do something similar, do it, but make sure you tell them they why they are getting the benefit and the value of it. In my experience, people don't value things they get for free. They only value it when they understand what the cost should have been. In addition to the meeting, we also gave a discount on their plan: a document we used to really help them see what they needed to do to create the future of their dreams.

You may be thinking, "I cannot afford to give some people a discounted fee or product?" If that's the case, you probably aren't charging enough in the first place. Even if you have to put your prices up to offset this discount to referrals, do it. These people are warmer, better clients than cold clients. They are less likely to mess you around, and they are more likely to become long term clients, so they deserve a discount.

In addition to asking for referrals, you need to make it part of your process, as otherwise it will get forgotten. We asked for introductions at the end of the second meeting, because that was the time where clients most bought into what we did. But it doesn't end there. We sent a sequence of letters after a client signed-up, and one of those specifically addressed the opportunity to introduce people to us, reminding clients that they also stood to benefit with a lovely dinner as a thank you. This acted as another opportunity for them to remember our request for an introduction.

If that's not enough, we also called a new client a couple of weeks after this meeting to check that their implementation was going smoothly, and to see if they had any questions. As well as being a great thing to do for the client relationship, this was another great opportunity to remind them about introducing us to people they knew.

What can you do in your business to allow you to get more referrals out of your existing customers? In my Better Future Framework, I get people to do an exercise called 'The Referral Revolution' to help them work on how they can generate more referrals in their business. You can find out more about this at **www.thetrusted.team/bff/**

## Become the Expert

*"An expert is a man who has made all the mistakes which can be made, in a narrow field." – Niels Bohr*

When I was travelling around the world, I played a lot of pool. As a kid, I loved playing snooker, occasionally heading to a snooker club with my Dad and my Uncle John. The smoky, dark and dingy atmosphere was like stepping into another world as a young man, even if I could only just reach the full-size snooker table.

At school we had a pool table back at the house, and I credit this table for inspiring my ability to eat quickly. Those who finished lunch first got back to house first, thus commanded the pool table. The love of playing pool then naturally migrated into pool in the pub when we were old enough, or snuck in underage. There is something quite beautiful in spending time playing pool with friends with a pint in your hand!

As a result of this misspent youth, I was pretty handy around a pool table. Pool served a great purpose when I was travelling on my own. It was my ticket to meet new people easily. I would head over to the table and plonk down some money to play the winner of the previous match. As long as I could win a few games, which I usually could, then by that point, I was in with a new group of friends. Whether in a surfer's bar in Bali, or an Aussie backpackers, a pool table was usually there for the taking.

When I was back in Queenstown, New Zealand, with Chris my best mate from school, and later my best man, we carried on that principle. Chris and I had played a lot of pool together over the years, so most evenings during our trip, we squeezed some pool in somewhere, but in New Zealand, they play to different rules. As you may know, in the UK, you generally get 2 shots if your opponent commits a foul. This is sufficient penalty to not foul on purpose, because 2 shots can allow a reasonable pool player to clear the table and not allow you back into the game. However, that is not the case in New Zealand.

In New Zealand, they do not give 2 shots in the event of a foul, instead they have a rule that prohibits deliberate fouls. This sounds logical, however given it is a question of someone's word, it is not always clear. Whether someone has played a foul shot intentionally or not is of course open to interpretation, and I was about to find that out.

Chris and I were drinking in Harry's Bar in Queenstown one evening, and saw that there was a pool competition. "That sounds like fun" we thought; a good way to meet a few of the locals, and to spice up the evening. We certainly got both. Chris got knocked out fairly early, but I made my way through to the final, so I was eager to find out who I was up against. I headed over to chat to the organiser of the competition to find out who I'd be playing against. Clad in baggy trousers and sporting dreadlocked hair, I was slightly concerned by his response. In a strong Kiwi accent, he said, "Dude, you'll be playing The Chief!

I headed over to the pool table where my battle with 'The Chief' was to take place. I was confronted by this huge 6ft 4 Māori man machine, wearing a sleeveless shirt to show off rippling muscles and tattoos. With his long hair and stone-cold face, he wouldn't have looked out of place in an All-Blacks shirt performing the Haka in front of the quivering opponents expecting their next pummeling. This wasn't someone you wanted to mess with, and his name 'The Chief' couldn't have been a more fitting description of him.

I actually got off to a pretty strong start in the game, despite the added nerves of it being a) a final and b) against 'The Chief'. I potted several balls with my first visit to the table, and was in a good position, but it was all about to change. The Chief had other ideas. 2 deliberate fouls in quick succession, and suddenly my back was against the wall. Chris, my wingman grabbed me and insisted I challenge him on these. After all, they were not in the spirit of the NZ game, and potentially, it should now be my game; but that involved confrontation. I had to call him on a deliberate foul, and that was clearly going to spark unrest. It was very easy for Chris to encourage my outburst, but he was not going to be on the other end of The Chief's wrath!

Despite my pride telling me to speak up and challenge The Chief, the self-preservation genes in my body were ensuring my lips stayed tightly shut. Not just because he was so intimidating, but because as a local these were his rules, and not mine. In the end I lost the game, and the tournament, solely, I believe, because of his underhand tactics. He walked out of Harry's that evening with the prize money, but at least I walked out without a bleeding nose and a black eye.

Now you may be wondering why I am telling you about playing pool against The Chief in Queenstown. Am I telling you this story because I want you to learn to speak up more? No. I am also not telling you because I want you to go to the gym more and wear sleeveless shirts and cover your arms with Māori tattoos. The reason I am telling you, is because I want you to become 'The Expert'. The reason I didn't challenge 'The Chief' was because he was 'The Expert'. Whilst I did not want to cross The Chief, had I wanted advice on how to win a pool tournament in NZ, he is exactly the person I would have gone to. Whilst his name didn't say it, his name to me was 'The Expert'.

In whatever it is you do, you need to become 'The Expert' too. By becoming 'The Expert' you will have people seek you out, and they will only want to deal with you. They will be knocking down a path to your door, instead of you having to try to find them. If I wanted to learn how to take the best freekicks in the world, I'd be seeking out David Beckham to teach me, as he is the expert in that field. If I wanted to play fly half for England and to kick them to world cup glory, I'd be seeking out Jonny Wilkinson's advice. If I wanted to win Wimbledon, I'd seek advice from Serena

Williams. If you can become the expert in your field, then you will have people seek you out to work with you.

There are lots of ways that you can become 'The Expert' in the eyes of your best fit clients, and what works best for you may be different to the next person, however there are some obvious routes to this regardless of your expertise.

The first, and in my eyes probably the best, is to become an author. Once I had 'The Dream Retirement: How to Secure Your Money and Retire Happy' published, I noticed a massive change in the way people perceived me.

At Efficient Portfolio we had a system, whereby, when a new client approached us, whether they were a referral, they found us online or they came to one of our workshops or dinners, we gave them 'The 15 Minute Free Finance Call'. We did this with anyone. This was done by one of the Financial Planners, and made sure that the potential client understood how we worked, and could make sure that were going to be able to help them. The main benefit of this call to us was to make sure that we were not wasting their time, but it also identified the best Financial Planner to help them.

One such example had come in as a client referral. They were a wealthy client, and with some complicated financial planning, so ordinarily they would have been booked in to see me, as the lead Financial Planner. My diary was extremely busy, and on this particular occasion, so was theirs, and it quickly became apparent that is was going to be extremely difficult for me to be able to look after them, so we booked the Exploration Meeting, with Tom, one of my other advisers. Extremely capable, they were in safe hands, but with more years' experience under my belt, ordinarily it would have been me doing the meeting.

These particular clients came to us having already read my book. Tom was going to be guiding them through The Efficient Wealth Management Process, but I wanted to ensure they knew I would be there in the background helping, so I sat in on the first 15 minutes of their Exploration Meeting. I felt guilty only being able to spend 15 minutes with them, however their perception was completely the opposite. They were extremely grateful that they got me for 15 minutes, and it caught me by surprise. In their eyes, I was the expert, the published author on the subject, and they were grateful to have my input on any level, and were delighted to have one of my team then look after them. In their eyes, I was the expert, and they didn't necessarily expect to then have access to me at all.

Therefore, if you want to become the expert in your field, one of the best ways you can achieve this is to write your own book. It doesn't even need to be the 90,000-word effort that became The Dream Retirement. In this book, I wanted to help people ensure they had enough money for the rest of their life, but also ensure that they created their life 2.0, the enhanced version of their life, both from the perspective of how they spend their time, and how they improve their health. A business book can be as little as 30,000 words, which actually isn't that much.

But if writing a book isn't for you, or the time to become an author isn't right, there are other ways to become an expert by producing other content. Write a blog or a newsletter, make videos or podcasts and share the content with people. More on that in the next section, but if people are regularly seeing you write or produce commentary on your specialist field, over time they will start to see you as the expert.

Another way to become the expert on your subject is to be speaking about it from a stage. Again, more on why you would want to do that later in the book, but if you are being asked to speak at events, you again will be seen as the expert.

Finally, the other way you can become the expert is to be featured in the media. Whether that be newspapers, the radio or on TV, being featured in the will massively raise people's perception of you, and you will rapidly become the expert in their eyes. The problem is that this isn't an easy thing to do. Unless you can identify your own very niche, it is difficult to get through the gatekeepers, and depending on your sector, even paying PR specialists is not always effective, as they need something compelling to work with.

One of the best ways to get asked to speak on other people's stages, and to be featured in the media, is to write your own book! Not only does this make you the expert in the eyes of your potential clients, it also has the same effect on people in the media. Since having The Dream Retirement published I have been invited to be on LBC radio on several occasions, been featured on ITV, I have been asked to speak at a variety of events, in front of thousands of people, and I have been the cover star of the leading financial services industry magazine. It makes everyone see you differently. I encourage you to write your own book and become the expert to your best fit clients.

You may be thinking, what on earth would I write a book about? One way to know this, is to start asking your clients the '1 year from now' question that we covered earlier in this chapter. Once you see a trend of what your best fit clients worries and opportunities are, therein lies the subject of your book. I saw that retirement worried people, so I wrote a book on how to create a dream retirement.

Another great thing about a book is that the content you write for it can also be used in a blog, newsletter and brochures. You could even turn it into other products like podcasts or an audiobook. It allows you to kill several birds with one stone.

You can of course do this the other way around. With my podcast, The Business of Endurance (**www.businessofendurance.co.uk**) I am currently transcribing the hours of content we have so that I can turn it into a book later this year.

I hope that you can create your own book, and you too can become the expert. To help you, I have created my own book writing exercise for you, so that you too can get those creative juices flowing. This can be found in the workbook on **www.thetrusted.team/books/entrepreneurial-happiness**

I also use an exercise at The Trusted Team called 'the Expert Accelerator', which achieves the same result. If you'd like a free copy, please email **hello@thetrusted.team**

Once done, I always turn this into a mind map that I can build up as I think of things. I find this really helpful to see the book structure, and also to identify the best place for things. Quite often moving content around on the mind map allows you to see better where which piece fits. Get creative, become an author, and please send me a copy of your new book when you get it!

## Attraction Marketing

If you want to gain more business opportunities, you need to attract them. Traditionally that would have meant paying for an advert in the newspaper, on the TV or on the radio. Whilst these are still viable options, they are expensive, and less effective than they have ever been, but whatever route you go down, you need Attraction Marketing Devices (AMD). An AMD is something we can give away for free, or for a relatively low price, that then directs people into your sales funnel.

I can offer them a free download of one of my books, and in exchange we will then send them a series of follow up emails that, whilst adding value to them by sharing ways they can overcome their problems and concerns, ultimately aims to get them contacting one of my businesses.

You need to have a number of AMD out there though. They can be a book, a white paper, a blog, a newsletter or a podcast. Anything you can give away for free to as many people as possible. Once people see the value you are creating, thus build a level of trust with you, you can then ask them to make a slightly bigger step that either involves a little more commitment or a cost.

Your AMDs need to point at your sales process, so you can then use your AMDs in your advertising, to draw people in. You are giving them stuff they value for free, and that makes the whole process far more effective. The question is, who are you targeting? Are they the right people? As a result, you need to have a clear picture of the type of people you are trying to attract.

In order that you can identify your best fit client, I have put together an exercise for you to work through. This can be found in The Entrepreneurial Happiness Workbook, that you can download for free from **www.thetrusted.team/books/entrepreneurial-happiness/**

Think about how you can advertise your business in the modern age. Create your own content that gives amazing value to your best fit clients, and share it through today's marketing channels. It maybe that you want to pay to advertise through Facebook, but by sharing engaging content though Facebook or LinkedIn, you can also achieve this for free. Maybe even a combination of the 2 would work even better. For example, we helped a number of farming clients that had sold land. I wrote a blog article on this subject, and that was put out there to other similar people.

## They Ask, You Answer
*"I wouldn't say I was the best manager in the business. But I was in the top one." Brian Clough*

I have read many marketing books, but far and away the best I have found is essentially about fibreglass pools sales.

'They Ask, You Answer' is by Marcus Sheridan, and is simply brilliant. The message is simple, but the results remarkably effective, and it fits perfectly into the concept of marketing yourself as the expert.

If you want to buy a swimming pool, what do you do nowadays? You go straight to Google and punch in a question. Maybe that is "What is the best type of pool for a garden", perhaps it's "Who is the best swimming pool company in my area" or potentially you might want a more specific answer like, "Which is better, a fibreglass pool or a concrete pool?" If a video entitled "What's the best swimming pool for you?" sits at the top of your Google search, followed by a list of articles about pools, what would you do? Probably click on the video. If there was a blog article at the top of your search entitled 'The best swimming pool company in your area', you'll click on that. As a consumer, you will have a question, and you want to find something that provides the answer.

Try asking a question Google (or any other search engine) about fibreglass pools, and I'm willing to bet you get an answer from River Pools and Spas- a company in Virginia USA. Sheridan was a founding director of River Pools and Spas, and with no previous marketing experience other than some training on the job, he sent them to the top of Google time and again. By doing so, he massively transformed their business, taking it from the brink of collapse to a highly successful company.

The principle is simple, and the book title says it all. What questions are your customers and clients asking?

Whatever they are, you need to be providing them with an answer online. Ideally, but not essentially, in the form of a video or blog. This is easy enough to achieve; you just need to answer your clients' and prospects' questions.

So, when you are doing any marketing ask yourself, think about what questions are my customers asking. Use the question as the title for your content, as Google, Bing and co. will love you for making their life easier, and if your web team can make sure it gets seen through Search Engine Optimisation, you'll be amazed at the results.

If you need help refining or finding your ideal client, why not book a free 1-hour coaching call with me/ I'd love to talk to you and show you the steps you need to take. To book, simply email me on **hello@thetrusted.team**

## Chapter Summary

- Boost the money flow into your business by generating more leads through initially by having an understanding of 'why' you do what you do, and then relaying that to your potential clients.
- Engage with your clients more and help them at a much deeper level by identifying what is important to them in the future, and then helping them achieve that using your expertise.
- Generate more referrals from your existing clients by exceeding expectations and implementing a structured referral process.
- Be seen by your clients and potential clients as 'The Expert' in order to be the only person they would come to for what you do. There are a variety of ways to do this, like blogs, Youtube and Social Media, but none better than writing your own book.
- You need to identify exactly what your best fit client looks like, and what their common concerns are, so that your marketing targets them with laser like focus.

# Chapter 5: 'Partnerships' with Purpose

*"Talent wins games, but teamwork and intelligence win championships."* Michael Jordan

The legend that was Steve Jobs is synonymous with the global giant that is 'Apple', but it's not the only household brand that he founded. In 1986, shortly after he was forced out of Apple, Jobs decided to go back to his roots and purchased a small, unknown computer manufacturer called 'Pixar' (yes, the one and the same). Wanting to completely overhaul the company, he relocated the business to an abandoned Del Monte canning factory, with the initial aim of creating three buildings, with offices for computer scientists, animators, and the executives. But Jobs quickly abandoned this plan, and decided against this segregation, instead creating one large collaborative space.

"The philosophy behind this design is that it's good to put the most important function at the heart of the building. Well, what's our most important function? It's the interaction of our employees. That's why Steve put a big empty space there. He wanted to create an open area for people to always be talking to each other." – Ed Catmull, the president of Pixar.

For Jobs, creating the space was largely irrelevant. His main aim was to achieve a collaborative culture, where everyone at Pixar could share ideas and inspire others. John Lasseter, the chief creative officer at Pixar, describes the equation this way: "Technology inspires art, and art challenges the technology."

So how did he achieve this? The answer is actually quite simple: Jobs moved the company mailboxes the meeting rooms, the cafeteria, the coffee bar, and the gift shop to the centre of the building, which he called 'The Atrium'.

Brad Bird, the director of "The Incredibles" and "Ratatouille," said, "The atrium initially might seem like a waste of space. But Steve realised that when people run into each other when they make eye contact, things happen."

This move certainly came at the expense of convenience, but Jobs' vision required consilience between all of Pixar's people, so the move was the best way to achieve his goal. Jobs believed that the pinnacle of creativity and productivity can only be achieved when there is a connection between everyone within a company, and I quite agree.

If you are running your business, or your own client base, do you ever feel that you are torn between spending time looking for new clients and working on the clients you have? If you constantly focus on the work in hand, you could risk not having any new business in the pipeline, and a few months down the line, you will have no work to do.

Conversely, if you focus too much of your attention on frantically generating an abundance of new clients, you'll have insufficient time to deal with the client work. As you can see, this is a bit of a dilemma!

Wouldn't it be brilliant if you had a team of people were always on the look-out for your best fit client? A team that were meeting lots of other people you don't know, but that knew in detail how you could help them, so that they could be spotting the opportunities for you. Sound expensive doesn't it, a bespoke sales team that it always out there finding clients for you and referring them into your business. What if I told you they could be free? Or alternatively, you only paid them when you successfully turned their referrals into clients? Hopefully that sounds even better. This was how we worked at Efficient Portfolio, and continue to do so at The Trusted Team, so I want to tell you how.

To use a financial example, most successful people need the help of an accountant, a solicitor and a Financial Planner at different stages in their life, as well perhaps some specialist advisers for their unique situation. Historically the client sat in the middle being given advice from the different sources. The accountant may be advising them to pay themselves a dividend as they have made good profits. The solicitor is helping them with organising their estate better, and the Financial Planner is advising them to fund their pension. The client is getting direction from the individual parties, but no one is looking at the bigger picture, except the client. There is no joined up approach, and they aren't looking at whether one set of advice is conflicting with another's because they appear to have different priorities.

In actual fact, there is a common thread running through this advice. If the increased profits are taken out of the business as a pension contribution, the client can save more Income Tax, but also protect more of their estate from Inheritance Tax. The client can also leave organise their Will so that their business shares are left to a Business Trust, to save further Inheritance Tax in the future, as well ensure that the assets pass down through the generations. This type of bigger picture planning requires the expertise of all 3 professions, so it is much better that they formulate a plan for the client together.

Instead of the client getting 3 sets of individual advice, the client gets better advice and also an easier life if these professional are talking to each other first, and then putting together a cohesive strategy that benefits the client the most. At Efficient Portfolio, where possible, we always tried to work closely with clients of other trusted advisers, so that we could formulate a plan that achieved all their objectives in the best possible way. We called working together in this way 'The Trusted Team Approach' (hence the name of the business that came after), and as a result we worked with a number of firms of accountants, solicitors and specialist advisers, to deliver a more comprehensive advice process for our clients. We were not looking to move them away from their existing advisers, simply to work more closely with them to ensure the client got the maximum value for their fees.

Whilst this is hopefully making logical sense, you may be wondering how this relates to your team of marketeers working around the clock to find you clients? One of the benefits to this approach is that you end up working with other firms that also look after your ideal clients, but that aren't competing with you. At The Trusted Team, for us that is typically accountants, web developers, HR consultants and other professional advisers- basically, anyone who provides a high-level service or guidance for business owners and entrepreneurs. Of course, that may not be the case for your business. So, the first step is to identify other businesses that share your best fit clients, but that are not competing with you in business.

The key to making this work is then in the next steps. It is relatively easy to find other firms that will agree to do this in concept, but much more difficult to then actually make it work. You need to establish what is in it for them.

You need to be clear what is in it for them. Is it adding value to their existing client service, a share of your fee or are they expecting referrals back? Make sure this is clear, and you can deliver, as sometimes it isn't easy to refer in the opposite direction. For example, the architect can refer work to a builder, but rarely the other way around, as that work has normally been done before the builder enters the conversation. If the architect expects the referrals back and doesn't get them, eventually they will stop referring clients to you, so you need to address this at the outset. Perhaps they don't want a fee share, and you cannot refer back, so find something else. Is it a day out, or offering your service for free? At The Trusted Team, for example, we offer our members a 10% reduction in their fees for every new client they introduce.

There is always something you can do, obviously taking care to avoid issues with the Anti-Bribery Act. If it is an activity or an experience, try and find something that allows you to build that relationship even stronger. A meal out, a day at the cricket/rugby, or maybe a game of golf all works well here but find something that works for you. The important thing is to establish what motivates your introducers to refer clients to you, and to make sure you deliver on that.

The next step of making sure The Trusted Team Approach works for you is to demonstrate exactly what you do. In the first instance this should be a presentation, already prepared, so that anytime you meet a potential Trusted Team partner, you can present them clearly exactly what you do. It never ceases to amaze me the number of business owners and professionals that I meet where very few have a professional presentation that can clearly show me.

You don't need to go through slide by slide, but having had a chat with them, you can use this as your visual material or as an aide memoir. This presentation should be 90% visuals, with only a few slides that have words on them. They don't want to sit and read in front of you, and if they are, they aren't listening to you talk! Work on the basis that nothing smaller than font 40, which will ensure you keep words to a minimum and pictures, graphics and charts make up the lion share of your work. After all, a picture tells a thousand words!

When you meet at a potential Trusted Team partner, there is also a clear structure that works well in the meeting. I call this The Trusted Team Meeting. Don't charge in guns blazing, desperate to get your presentation done and your polished pitch out there. Firstly, they may be thinking the same, which means they aren't listening, and secondly, until you know more about them, how can you appeal to their greatest needs? Think back to Sir Alex Ferguson and Gazza, and the R-Factor Question® from Strategic Coach® - "If we were sat here 1 year from now, what must have happened for you to be happy with the progress you have made?"

If, for example, you know they really want to grow their practice income, then guess what, you offering an introducer fee for referrals may well be their ticket to get there. We have also found it very helpful to have a brochure they can take away specifically aimed at 'The Trusted Team'. They'll probably chuck it without reading it, but the quality of this brochure it will give them a feel for the quality of the work you will be giving to their clients, so don't scrimp on this. Make it look professional. If you have written a book, make sure you give them a signed copy of that too. After all, it makes you 'The Expert!'

The Trusted Team Meeting is a powerful start, and if you stop there, you may leave the meeting thinking you have cracked the nut, with the promise of a consistent flow of referrals. In my experience though, it rarely is enough. If you want to really make this a roaring success, there are a few more things you need to do.

The first is you need to make this a more compelling offer for their clients. To go back to my former financial planning firm as an example, the first meeting with a Financial Planner was called 'The Exploration Meeting', and normally cost the client £197 if they came to us cold. However, if they came to us as an introduction from one of our Trusted Team Partners, then we knew they were more likely to be a better fit for our business. As a result, we waived the cost of this meeting. That means the Trusted Team Partner could genuinely say to their clients that as a result of them referring the client to us, the client would save £197. That made the Trusted Team Partner look great in the client's eyes, and also made it more compelling for the client to follow their suggestion of meeting us. Win, win!

Secondly, when you meet The Trusted Team Partner, just being told about what you can do for their clients is not enough. It is much more powerful if they see it first-hand. I'll come back to 'The Unique Business Process' later in this book, so I won't go into detail here, but if it's appropriate, you need to get them to go through part or all the way through your Unique Business Process if at all possible.

At Efficient Portfolio, the second stage of our Unique Business Process was called 'The Efficient Financial Plan': A bespoke plan that allowed clients to understand more about their current finances, see what their financial future would look like, and clearly understand what actions they could take to turn that financial future into the one they wanted. We charged between £500 and £3,000 for The Efficient Financial Plan, so it was a valuable document.

The best way for us to show a potential future Trusted Team Partner how we could help their clients, was to show them how we could help them. So, in addition to offering the partner a free Exploration Meeting, worth £197, we offered them, and their other business partners, a free Efficient Financial Plan too, worth up to £3,000. That way they got to witness first-hand how we could improve what they were currently doing, how much clarity a Lifetime Cash-Flow Forecast could give them about their own financial future, and why we were different to any firm they have dealt with in the past.

This approach has 2 advantages: Firstly, if your introducers understand how your Unique Business Process helped them, they can better explain it to their clients, and can even honestly say that they have been through it themselves; secondly, if the introducers like what you do and your advice is relevant to them, there is a fair chance that they will go onto become a client of yours too. You can still charge them for this, as this is generally where you start incurring the bigger costs and taking on much greater liability, so you don't necessarily want to be doing that without charging, but it will of course depend on your business.

Maybe you can charge them, but favourable rates, but if they end up becoming a client or customer of yours as a result of liking what you do, that makes them even more likely to refer their clients to you. Not just because they understand it and see the benefit of what you do, but because they are probably now seeing you on a regular basis.

The next step to make this new Trusted Team relationship work is to follow on from that last point. Arrange regular times to meet to discuss hot topics in your business, any mutual clients that you have referred, and also importantly case studies. If you bring a case study of a client you have helped, and they do the same, it gives you a great understanding of the ways that they/you can help other clients.

These regular meetings are then the springboard onto finding some new referrals for each other. We all know that normally following a meeting, we will all have an inbox full of emails, and a pile of work on our desks, so having to think up clients to refer would ordinarily take pride of place in the back seat, soon to be forgotten. Identifying specific actions and specific people in the meeting will mean that we can all focus our attention on the most important actions, which will lead to much greater success. So, schedule in these regular meetings. I aim to do them quarterly with our Trusted Team partners, to ensure the Trusted Team relationship blossoms, otherwise it will wilt and die.

Another way to really get this working well for you is to identify how you can give value back to your Trusted Team Partners. One way I have done this was by creating 'The Breakthrough Business Breakfast'. This was a free monthly breakfast meeting where I taught other business professionals, particularly accountants and solicitors, how they could find more clients, have a better work life balance and enjoy their careers more. In essence, it was the first incarnation of my coaching company.

At 'The Breakthrough Business Breakfast' events I got to share with my Trusted Team Partners the sort of ideas that I am sharing with you in this book, but I could also do more. It is one thing reading a book, but working with the author in a workshop format takes it to a whole new level. I know this from attending the Tony Robbins events, as an example. The learning and ideas that spring from attending an event are far greater than you get when you read a book.

In addition to thinking about how you can improve your own business, you can hear some of the ideas of like-minded professional peers, and that can inspire you into new ideas too. It is also an opportunity to network with other business owners, and to extend your own Trusted Team network. If you'd like to see this in practice, why not join us for a free taster workshop? It's a jam-packed day of coaching, networking and innovation. To find our when the next taster is taking place, please email **hello@thetrusted.team**

The final step to really make this relationship flourish is plan some joint events together and initiatives together. That could be a golf day, a seminar, or a marketing exercise. If you have written your book, why not offer to give your Trusted Team free copies of the book that they can send to their clients as a gift. It makes them look good, and simultaneously they are sending around your 'big business card'. Another win, win situation!

The key to a strong Trusted Team relationship is finding those mutually beneficial situations. If in business you can find these moments, everyone walks away happy and motivated. If you drive too hard a deal, or like the builder and the architect expect it all one way, the relationship will soon fizzle out. Find the win, wins, and you will make a huge success. In my Better Future Framework, I get people to do an exercise to help them identify the members and the approach to use for their very own Trusted Team. You can find out more about this at **www.thetrusted.team/bff/**

In my 3 Steps to Entrepreneurial Happiness virtual workshop, I also talk people through the 'Partnership Playbook' tool, which will help on this topic. If you'd like to join this free, online event, please visit **www.thetrusted.team/virtual-workshops/**

When you have other business owners and professionals on the lookout for your next clients, it really does oil the cogs of your business beautifully!

## Chapter Summary

- Identify other businesses that have the same clients as you, but that aren't in competition with you.
- Work out what it is they are most looking for.
- Build a Trusted Team of other business professionals so that you can create a far better solution for your clients, as well as refer clients to each other.
- Find ways to add as much value as possible to your Trusted Team to make the referrals flow.

# Chapter 6: Business by 'Numbers'

*"Where attention goes, energy flows."* Tony Robbins

A few summers ago, a friend of mine, Dave, was over from the states. As an avid baseball and basketball fan, he asked if I would take him to a great British sporting event. As it was during the summer my options were limited, but I could get tickets to see England play in a One Day International at cricket. What better demonstration of a truly British sporting occasion? Lunch hamper in hand, I was confident he would enjoy this great British sporting day out.

We arrived at our seats just in time for the first over, having detoured via the bar to secure a drink to wash down our smoked salmon sandwiches and Melton Mowbray Pork Pie. The sun was shining, and England were bowling; this was going to be a great day.

It was shortly after the first over that he spotted the score board. In a way that only an American could, he blasted, "What the hell is that thing when it's at home? Is that telling me the stats for the whole damn season?"

Have you ever seen a professional cricket scoreboard? If you follow cricket, the scoreboard makes complete sense. You know how many overs have been bowled and how many are left in the innings; you know which batsmen are in, how many runs they've scored, who's facing the next ball and how many more they need to win; you know the bowler's name, the number of balls left in the over, the runs scored and the wickets lost. All crucial information about the match that tells you who's winning, but to Dave, it was like looking at a Japanese textbook on brain surgery. He couldn't read the scoreboard, so he couldn't understand what was happening in the game!

Business is the same as sport, and particularly cricket: If you can't read the scoreboard, you don't know the score, and if you don't know the score, how can you tell who are the winners from the losers?

Many business owners I meet cannot read and understand their accounts. If they cannot read and understand their accounts, then they don't know what is going on. They don't know the score, and they don't know whether they are winning or losing. As a result, if you run your own business it is essential that you at least have a grasp of your balance sheet and your profit and loss. Even better though is to track your income versus your expenditure.

However, this chapter, and section of The BFF system, isn't about knowing how to read your balance sheet and P&L, as important as that is. It is about knowing your most important numbers to your specific business, and not 3 months or even 12 months after the event, but knowing them now.

Looking at your accounts 3 or even 6 months after the year has finished is a bit like trying to make a substitution half an hour after the game of cricket has ended. You could well have already lost the game by that stage. Even reviewing your accounts every 3 months with your accountant just isn't enough. That's like only assessing the game at half time and full time. You need to have your finger on the pulse of the game, and to do that you need weekly reporting of all your key results.

One of the times I was lucky enough to hear Sir Clive Woodward, the England Rugby World Cup winning manager speak, he talked about the impact that Prozone had on the England team. This was a system that gave him live data on all the England players on the pitch: Who was running the most, who was making the most tackles, and who was not performing as well as they might. After reviewing the first game it was used in, Sir Clive couldn't understand why Will Greenwood, one of the England backs that is known as being a bit of a joker, kept running sideways while the ball was in the scrum, i.e. nowhere near him. At one stage Sir Clive thought perhaps he had a niggling injury and might have to take him off, but he seemed to be moving ok when he got the ball. After the game, Sir Clive collared Will and asked him, "What was with the sideways running? Did you have a muscle strain?" Will replied, "No governor, I just wanted to be the player that had covered the most ground on Prozone!"

Will Greenwood aside, what Prozone gave Sir Clive was live data on what was happening on the pitch. He puts the introduction of this live data as one of the key differentiating factors in why they went on to win the World Cup. So, if you want to win the game of business, you too need live, up to date and accurate data.

Whether you run your own company or are a partner or consultant in a bigger company, you need to know what you most important numbers are, and you need to keep track of them on a weekly basis. Let me explain what I mean.

As I mentioned, at Efficient Portfolio we built clients an Efficient Financial Plan- their own bespoke document that contained analysis of their investments to see what was good and what was not. It also contained a Lifetime Cash-Flow Forecast that allowed them to see what their financial future currently looked like, and then provided recommendations of what they needed to do to achieve their goals. After our first meeting with the client we built this plan for them and it usually took us around three months to complete. Once the client had read it, we met them again and made sure they understood everything; sometimes this took an additional meeting or two to get everything finalised. Sometimes it then took us up to three more months to implement their wishes. That meant that it could be up to nine months before we got to the end of that client journey, and also nine months before we got the lion share of our fees.

As a result of this time frame, it was very easy to get caught up in what client work was happening at that time. For example, one of the advisers may have seen a lot of new clients in January; in March they were busy reviewing the clients' finances; in April they were busy helping the Paraplanner finish all the Efficient Financial Plans; in May they were busy conducting the Planning Meetings; in July they were busy implementing the clients' desired outcomes; and then in September, they had nothing to do! That is unless they knew their numbers. If they knew how many Exploration Meetings they needed to do every week and every month, they knew how to keep their client pipeline full. If they knew what the average client brought in in fees in their first year, they knew how many Planning Meetings they needed to have booked each month to hit their target.

But it doesn't stop there: Once the planning was agreed with the client, we sent a Suitability Letter to confirm exactly which parts of the planning the client wanted to implement. If these started to build up, because the team were busy, this could have been a compliance problem for the business, so as the business owner I needed to know what that number was. Is it rising or falling? Was the weekly income more than the weekly expenditure this year, and how had that trend changed over the last quarter or year? After all, 'turnover is vanity, profit is for sanity, and cash-flow is reality'! Which were the best months on average, and which were the worst? Were complaints and quibbles becoming more of a problem? Was our customer satisfaction score rising or falling?

If you don't know the score, you don't know whether you are winning or losing. If you don't even have a scoreboard, what hope have you got of knowing the score? As a result, you need to track your key business figures. Not on an annual basis through your accountant, because by the time you see that, it is too late. Even on a quarterly basis you are behind the times. You need to track these numbers on a weekly basis, so you can rectify problems immediately and maximise opportunities before they are lost.

To this day, one of my first jobs every Monday morning is to review our Successful Business Scoreboard. It tells me nearly everything I need to know about each of my businesses in one line of data. It allows me to see whether the businesses are on track to hit its targets, and, if not, why. It allows me to see the length of the 'sausage machine', it gives me the ability to predict cash-flow and business in the months ahead, and it enables me to spot problems that may be building in the background.

If you want to win at business, you need to know your numbers. You need to know, keep track, and review your numbers every week, as this will put you in the driving seat of your business.

Your numbers may well be different to mine. You probably have a completely different business model to me, but you will have key stages in your client journey that you can track, ways you can track whether you are getting better or worse, and ways that you can see whether you are making more or less money than before. I have put a lot of time into refining mine, and it has evolved into a key part of our businesses. Later in this chapter I'll show you how to create your very own Successful Business Scorecard, using mine as a template, but before we get to that stage, we need to know what your numbers are, so it's worth grabbing a pen and paper and starting to think about these now. This isn't about creating a huge and burdensome admin exercise for you, so please don't worry.

I'd like you to identify what are your key numbers. What do you need to keep track of to ensure you know how your business is running? Not only do you need to identify what numbers you need to know, you need to identify who in your team can track and complete these figures for you on a weekly basis. Finally, you also need to identity a target for each number. Ideally, this should be a calculated figure, however you may not be able to do this at this stage.

Here is an example. We need to keep track of how many referrals we get, how many first meetings we generate from these leads, and how many of them become clients. Moreover, we also need to know how many new client meetings and referrals we need to hit our target.

If our year's target is £1m of client fee income, and the average new client generates us £10,000 in fees in their first year, I know that to hit our target we need to be writing £19,230 worth of business each week. That means we need to take on roughly two new clients a week. But not everyone we meet becomes a client. I know that around 73% of first meetings yield new clients, as I have been tracking this for some time, so I now know that I actually need 2.7 meetings per week to hit that. Of the referrals we get from different sources, I know that we convert 55% of them into meetings As a result, I know that if I want to write £1m of new business, I don't need 2.7 referrals per week, I actually need 5.

The great thing about this is that next year, if my target is £2m, unless I can generate more income per client, or improve those percentages, I know I now need to be generating 10 new referrals per week. Of course, you need to do both, and we'll come to that is due course, but at this stage, it is about knowing the score!

When you come to set your targets, you can either decide on how you can calculate a more specific target that will deliver the results you want, or initially this can be a gut feeling for what you think you need to achieve in that area to hit your annual targets. In time, as you track the numbers more closely, you will be able to set more accurate targets that will deliver the results you desire.

I hope you enjoy creating your very own Successful Business Scorecard.

Rome wasn't built in a day. I am on about our 7$^{th}$ version of our Successful Business Scorecard. It is ever evolving. Not only that, just by writing this section of the book I have just identified another way we can make it even better. The clarity you will get on your business by looking at these figures each week is quite amazing. In less than 5 minutes you can see every important aspect of your business and identify what needs to happen for it to hit your annual targets and to get back on track if you are off. It will allow you to identify problems building in the business far earlier than before, and make sure you always have your finger on the pulse. In time, it will also allow you to work fewer hours and in a more flexible way, so you could also create a win, win situation.

In addition to knowing your numbers, you need to know where your referrals and clients and customers are coming from. We have a document that we call 'The Referral Register. It is really powerful and important to be able to look back and see where all of your clients are coming from. Were they referrals from clients, from introducers, from seminars, from your website? By knowing where your new clients are coming from, you can track which of your strategies is proving successful. There is no point in ploughing good money after bad, or spending time with people who are not generating you the clients you thought they would.

Keeping track of where your referrals come from is really important, but to be really successful we need to take it a step further. We need to look at where our best 5 clients each year came from. Take a look at the total earnings from your clients over the last 12 months and identify where each of them came from. This is important for a couple of reasons.

Firstly, if you are getting your very best clients from one or two sources, you perhaps need to spend even more time nurturing those sources. If it is a particular introducer, could you spend more time with them to get even more of those best fit clients? Could you take them out to dinner to thank them? If it is your website that is converting well, how could you get that in front of more people's eyes?

The second reason is it is important to know what the average earnings from your 5 best clients were. It is sensible to track this every year, so go back and look at how this changed in recent years. I hope you find it is getting higher each year. If it isn't, then perhaps you need to look into how you could make that figure higher next year?

Now you know the average fee earned from your top clients over the last year, the final piece of the puzzle is to set you minimum client fee. It is often difficult when you meet some that isn't your best fit client to say no. An example in my financial planning business was that Henry, one of the Financial Planners at Efficient Portfolio, saw a client that really couldn't afford to pay us for the advice he needed. Henry decided to waive the cost of our Efficient Financial Plan, in the hope that he would still get a £1500 fee if the client wanted us to help him reorganise his pensions. As he said to me afterwards, having invested the time in doing the Exploration Meeting, and paid the cost of the marketing to attract him, it makes sense to try and cover our costs by trying to generate £1500 out of this client.

The problem is that this client would cost us a lot more than £1500. The marketing cost and adviser time had already been lost. You need to look forwards not backwards. If Henry did the plan for free, and even if he generated £1500 in fee income, it would have cost us money. For the work that was needed to build the plan, to implement the ideas, to pay the Professional Indemnity Insurance and regulatory fees associated with the advice, and the other costs associated with this work, it would have easily amounted to £1500; however, that isn't the biggest problem. For every bit of time Henry spent looking after this client, that was time taken away from him where he could have been finding his best fit client. Whilst the £1500 may have meant we broke even, it would more than likely have cost us around £10,000 in fees, as he would not have found someone that was a best fit client in that time.

You may be thinking at this stage what a cruel and heartless person Charlie is. That client needed their help, but could not afford it, and therefore they were going to shun him. Let's be honest, we are in business to make money. If we don't make money, we won't be here to help anyone. That said, that doesn't mean you shouldn't do some pro-bono work as a way of giving back. We do this across all of our businesses; however, it is important we do it on a pre-determined number of occasions, otherwise we would run the risk of running our business dry and not making any profit.

In my Better Future Framework, I get people to do the 'Successful Business Scorecard' exercise to help them work on what that should look like. You can find out more about this at **www.thetrusted.team/bff/**

One number that you should track on your Successful Business Scorecard is your time off. Later on in this book I'll tell you how to achieve more whilst working less, but for now remember that what is measured gets done, so make sure you know where you currently are.

You can download a copy of The Successful Business Scorecard, which includes my Referral Register, from **www.thetrusted.team/sbs/** If this proves as invaluable to your business as it has ours, please email me to tell me at **charlie@thetrusted.team** . I'd love to hear your success stories.

## Chapter Summary

- It is vital you have your finger on the pulse of your business. If you don't know the score, you don't know if you are winning or losing.
- Create a Successful Business Scorecard so that you know exactly what is happening in your business.
- You need to know what minimum fee income you will work for, plus also what fees your best clients are generating for you, so you can move the business forward in the way you want.
- Create a 'Death-List', so you know whether you are on track to hit your targets for the year ahead and can adapt early enough if not.

# Chapter 7: Amass Your Wealth

*"If you fail to plan, you are plan to fail."* Benjamin Franklin

The final step to The Profitable Business PLAN is to 'Amass' as much of the money that you make as possible. It is all very well finding ways to make lots more money, but only if you then use it wisely will it allow you to create the future you want, both for you and your business. If you end up handing over huge chunks to the tax man, to below average financial products and to poor Financial Advisers, your efforts will be wasted.

Making the most of your money used to be my bread and butter. I love helping people like you improve your business, and one of the greatest ways I can do this is by sharing my expertise around creating a better financial future for you and your loved ones. I realise as a business owner you are often so focused on making money within your business, you give the money you make, and particularly the money you have withdrawn from the business, even less attention. We need to change that now.

You know your business, but do you understand how to make the most of your money? You may have a pension, and maybe even a Financial Adviser, but do you know whether you are on track to have enough money for the future you want? Will you be able to afford to retire when and how you want to? Will you be able to afford to fulfil the bucket list goals that you have been promising yourself? Will you be able to afford to live where you want to in retirement? Will you be able to afford to pass your business down to the next generation if they want to be involved?

Will you be able to create a legacy, rather than just leaving a few items in a Will?

I don't want this chapter to be a long account of all the financial things you need to do to create your dream retirement. After all, that is why I wrote my first book, 'The Dream Retirement: How to Secure Your Money and Retire Happy.' If you want to download it for free, you can do so at **www.thetrusted.team/books/** . I realise that downloadable copies aren't as good as the real thing though. They just aren't as nice to read, and you cannot scribble on them either. As a result, I also give a number of free physical copies away each month, so if you send me an email at **charlie@thetrusted.team** and ask, I'll perhaps even stick a physical copy in the post for you too!

This chapter isn't a comprehensive account of what you can do with your money. As I am now a former Financial Planner, not a practicing one, I certainly don't want this to be taken as advice! Instead, it is designed to be more about the concepts around what you need to do to become financially free in the future and provide you with some general guidance- a financial education, if you will. There are some amazing opportunities that only a business owner has, so I'll highlight these along the way. Finally, I don't want you to think that implementing all this stuff needs to take up a lot of your time. In fact, later this chapter I'll show you how you can take a huge stride to improving your financial future in just 2 minutes.

I started my career in financial services in 1999 and left it, partially behind, in 2023. During my time in the industry, I discovered that there are 6 key steps to creating and maintaining a truly happy financial future. They are as follows:

### 1. Prepare

Prepare, not repair!

Would you agree that the current £ 221.20 a week (correct as of April 2024) that the government provides you with in retirement is not going to be enough to live on in retirement? In fact, imagine trying to live your current lifestyle on that amount of money? If you do not save enough for your retirement, that is what is going to end up happening to you.

And here's the thing my former industry really isn't very good at teaching people, and that's the psychology or mechanism around saving, which is probably one the keys to your success. Financial Advisers will tell you that you need to save and to set up a pension, but they often don't tell you the secrets to amazing financial success, which is all about the systems and psychology you use, not the products. Good financial planning is also about mitigating the risks of unexpected events that can derail your plan in the future.

At Efficient Portfolio I created **The S.M.A.R.T. Saving Solution** to ensure our clients could prepare properly for their retirement. This was how we helped our clients build their very own **S.I.M.P.L.E. Money Management Method**- a system that allowed them to ensure that they were saving the right amounts for different areas of their life in a nearly effortless way that made the maximum impact on their lifestyle and future.

In order to get to financial freedom as quickly as possible, you need to understand a number of key financial principles; an example of this is compound growth. Let me explain with a story. Chris my best man lives in Singapore. When he was over a few years ago, so we said we would go and swing the clubs in anger and play some golf. Having not seen each other for a while, there was the usual banter flying around- you know the sort of thing; I'd say, "You know your problem is that you stand too close to the ball…. after you've hit it". He'd come back with; "It's a dead sheep… still ewe!"

Anyway, Chris is an investment banker, so as the reputation goes, is a little reckless with money. On the other hand, I need to be cautious with money. Walking up the first tee Chris said we ought to be playing this golf match for money. "Chris", I said, "I do not need any extra reason to play bad golf, so please, let's not."

" Charlie," he retorted, "You are a successful businessman, and I am sure you can cope with playing golf for a little money!"

"If we must, but let's just play for 10p per hole."

"10p per hole sounds a little pathetic," he says, "Let's do that but double it each hole".

"Ok", I reluctantly agreed.

On the first hole, which I think I lost, we were playing for 10p, but hey, as he says, I'm a successful businessman, and I'm sure I can cope with that. On the second hole we were playing for 20p, not too much stress there either. 40p on the $3^{rd}$ and 80p on the fourth are also fine with me. By the

7th though I am starting to shake over the puts a little, as we are now playing for £6.40 a hole, but I am playing reasonable golf, so I am confident I can take it off him. However, it quickly starts getting out of hand from here on in.

By the 10th we were playing for £51 per hole, and that was too much for me, so I called the betting a day, but it certainly made me think about what was going to happen if we continued. By the 16th we would have been playing for £3,276, and on the 18th we would have been playing for £13,107! Despite the earlier machismo, this was way too big for either of us to be entertaining.

The increasing amounts I've just told you about is what is known as compound growth. It is the effect of the growth on the growth on the growth. To look at it another way, if you look a standard piece of paper (0.05mm thick) and folded it in half 50 times, do you know how high it would reach? The answer is about 100 million kilometres, which is about two thirds of the distance between the Sun and the Earth. Amazing isn't it! That is compound growth at work. If you can get your money benefiting from compound growth, you will reach financial freedom more quickly, and stay there for longer, so you need to find ways to get a bit more growth out of your money at every opportunity.

As a business owner you have some unique opportunities, and also some unique risks. For example, you can extract money direct from your company into your pension, and save paying Income Tax, Corporation Tax and National Insurance Tax on this money. You can use the money in your pension to purchase a commercial property that you can rent back to your business, which means that your company is then paying rent to your pension. That pension is also secure in the situation where your business runs into financial difficulty. Your pension can loan money back to your company, and it can also borrow.

As a business owner you can control the amount of tax you pay through the amount and structure of your drawings, and you can use investment tax wrappers to shelter larger drawings from the tax man. You can leave money in the business and benefit from Entrepreneur's Relief or reduce your tax by drawing the money out at a lower rate once you have retired. You have flexibility to create an amazing financial strategy to get you to financial freedom as quickly as possible, and give you the opportunity to stop working, if you wish!

However, as a business owner you have more risks than an employee. For example, if you are sick, have an accident or even worse, die, you need to ensure that you and your loved ones have enough money for their future. That needs to be income to pay the bills, whatever they are, and capital to pay for upfront costs. One of the most valuable things I did as a Financial Planner was to help our clients see the financial shortfalls they had and fill those gaps with the necessary protection.

In addition to these though the business owner has other considerations to think about. What happens if a key member of staff suffers the same fate? Could your opportunity to hit your targets be lost? Could key relationships be lost if that were to happen, with clients or even your bank? Key Person Protection ensures you have the means to deal with these scenarios, if they occur.

Also, do you own the business with someone else? If they die and leave their shares to their partner, children or parents, how will that affect your business? Do you want to run the business with their beneficiary, and do they even want to be in that situation? Ideally you want to buy them out, but will you have the funds? If the boot was on the other foot, wouldn't your beneficiary want the money rather than the shares? Shareholder Protection or Partnership Protection makes sure who needs the shares gets them, and who needs the money gets that.

## 2. Plan

If you are failing to plan, you are planning to fail!

Probably the biggest concern people have in the lead up to retirement is the uncertainty over whether they will run out of money later on in life. Another key concern is not knowing if they will be able to do the things they want to. On the flip side of that is feeling too worried to spend, thus ending up becoming the richest person in the graveyard.

The key to a successful retirement is being able to look into the future, see what you need, and then plan how you can get there, including what you can afford today. 'A goal is just a dream with a deadline' and that could not be more poignant than when it comes to retirement.

You'd think this would be covered by most Financial Advisers, but it generally isn't. Financial Advisers tend to focus on the products, and the advice around them. However, a small minority of the financial services industry, at the point of writing, has taken this a huge step further and embraced financial planning.

When I first moved to London after coming back from travelling, 2 girl friends and I decided we were going to head down to Brighton for the weekend in search of a party. Before you question my morals, these were friends who were girls, not 2 girlfriends! This was well before Sat Navs and Google Maps on your phone had been invented, so we would have normally reverted to more traditional paper-based navigation, but for whatever reason I didn't have a road atlas in my car. I had achieved a Gold Duke of Edinburgh Award only a few years before, so with my orienteering skills and an air of confidence, off we went. We set off from Chiswick, in West London, and aimed south. The road signs would surely lead us straight there, or so we thought.

My passengers didn't offer me much assistance, and we managed to get off to a pretty bad start. We found the M3 and headed out of London, thinking that would get us on the right route. The signposts implied that the road would take us to Portsmouth, and we knew that was on the south coast, so we couldn't go too far wrong with that as a starting point. The problem was that the further we got on this route, the more damage we did to our overall. We concluded that the M3 was taking us too far west and decided to try an easterly cross-country detour. After driving for more than an hour and a half, when the total journey should take about an hour and a half, we accepted defeat. Eventually we stopped at a garage and bought a map, whilst also asking for clarity where we actually were. A rather amused cashier pointed at Portsmouth, and then showed us the correct road to Brighton.

By this point, we had gone so far off route that it took us another 1 ½ hours to get to Brighton, by which point we had missed half of the party! The mistake we made was that we didn't plan the route beforehand, and we didn't have anything to ensure we kept on track.

Nowadays, as an organised dad, I would have looked at the route in advance on Google Maps to give me a good idea of where we were heading and the time it would take, and then used a Sat Nav to keep us on track and make adjustments to any errors we made or diversions around any road closures. Why am I telling you this? Well, the approach we took on that ill-fated jaunt to Brighton is the approach that most people take to their finances. They only look at the next road sign, not the bigger picture.

This sounds obvious doesn't it, but in actual fact most people spend their life managing their finances in this way. Most people go through their life not really knowing what their financial future looks like. They can see what they have now, and how their decisions have affected their money in the past by looking in the rear-view mirror, but they do not look further ahead. In order to get to your destination, you need to plan the journey at the start, so you have an idea of how you are going to get there. Ideally, you then need a Sat Nav or a map to ensure you keep looking at the bigger picture to make sure you arrive safely.

As a result, when it comes to their finances, people get lost, and most don't get to where they wanted to go. Where they do end up isn't where they wanted to be at all, because of the odd wrong turn along the way and they end up in Portsmouth instead of Brighton. Whilst they are not a million miles away from where they wanted to be, to undo those wrong turns isn't quick and easy. With your money this could mean that you run out during your lifetime, or you could die the richest person in the graveyard, leaving your children with a big Inheritance Tax bill, and having not done many of the things you always wanted to do.

When it comes to your finances, what is your Sat Nav or your map? It is known as a Lifetime Cash-Flow Forecast. A Lifetime Cash-Flow Forecast gives you the clarity of what your financial future will look like. It projects your life forward allowing you to build in the aspects that are important to you, so that you can see how they will impact your financial future. It allows you to make more informed decisions because you can see the impact they will have on your future.

To allow you to see where you are going with your money, it isn't just a case of removing the blindfold or looking forwards out of the window screen. You need to imagine that your life, from here to the end, is a timeline.

Lifetime Cash-Flow Forecasting enables you to visualise your future wealth, and see how the decisions you make today will affect your wealth over time. It is vital in financial planning, as it helps you gain greater clarity around your financial future.

The Lifetime Cash-Flow Forecast gives you clarity on your financial future, but that is just one piece of the jigsaw. In order to help our clients see their financial future more clearly, we created **The S.A.F.E. Retirement Roadmap** so that we could help them clarify what their financial future looked like, and to be able to forecast different scenarios, because this gave them the confidence to make the right financial decisions for their desired future. Do you think you would benefit from knowing more clearly about your financial future? If you do, we also built a more basic version of the Lifetime Cash-Flow Forecast that you can play around with for free at **www.efficientportfolio.co.uk/tools/life-time-cash-flow-forecast/**.

If you would like our help to build you a much more detailed Lifetime Cash-Flow Forecast, that takes account of all your specific finances now, and the different scenarios you want to consider for your future, please get in contact with us by emailing us at **hello@efficientportfolio.co.uk**.

Whilst we no longer provide financial planning ourselves, we still help people by connecting them with expert Financial Planners. We believe that clients must be placed at the heart of every financial planning strategy, and that building a deep understanding of what you want to achieve in the future and what concerns you have about the present is the only way to truly reach your financial objectives. That is why we only work in conjunction with FCA Regulated Financial Advisers and Financial Planners who believe in these principles, and have demonstrated the highest level of qualification, ethics and have tried and tested client relationship practices.

**The S.A.F.E. Retirement Roadmap** is, however, about much more than just The Lifetime Cash-Flow Forecast. That is the cornerstone of it, but it is also about better understanding your current finances, i.e. what bits are good, and what bits aren't, and therefore need improving. It is also looking into the future, because only once you have a clear idea of what you want in the future, a Financial Planner can really help.

So, let's take a look at what is important to you in the future.

In order that you can create a better financial future, I have put together an exercise for you to work through. This can be found in The Entrepreneurial Happiness Workbook, that you can download for free from **www.thetrusted.team/books/entrepreneurial-happiness/**

### 3. Profit

Growth over and above inflation!

Saving money is important, but if you do not get that money working harder for you, then you will have to save twice as much, for twice as long and it will run out twice as quickly, so you need to allow your savings to generate a profit. What do I mean by 'Profit'? No, not the same as profit for your business, but similar. There is a saying that 'turnover is vanity, but profit is sanity.' The same applies to your personal money.

Surprisingly, the amount of interest or growth you are getting is not the important figure. The essential figure is how much more growth/interest are you getting above inflation. If you are getting 8% growth that may sound brilliant, but if inflation is 10%, you just lost 2% of your money. If you get 3% growth on your money, that may sound rubbish, but if inflation was negative at -2% deflation, you just got 5% growth, which may well be good for you. What I therefore mean by profit, in this instance, is getting your money to grow faster than inflation.

That means that the buying power is going down every year. As a result, you need to get that money working hard for you, rather than you working harder for it! You need to be benefiting from as much growth as possible to get the process of compound growth really working for you, as I pointed out earlier in this chapter.

At Efficient Portfolio I created **The R.A.D.I.C.A.L. Investment Approach**- a 7-step process that helped our clients feel more confident that they were getting the best returns possible, for a level of risk that they are comfortable with. Ensuring their money was growing over and above inflation, but without gradually getting risker and risker, as happens naturally in a portfolio, was critical.

As a business owner, this doesn't just apply to the money you have extracted from your business into your pension or your own savings and investments. Most successful businesses retain a level of capital in the company they never really intend to use, just in case they need it in the future. This money usually sits in a bank account doing nothing apart from being eroded by inflation over time. Whilst it is important to seek advice for your specific situation, there is usually no reason not to invest some of this money to ensure that it is at least keeping pace with inflation, if not growing above it.

### 4. Pension

Creating a dynamic income that matches your lifestyle!

As and when you get to retirement, you need to turn the capital you have saved into an income. You could of course hand all those savings over to one company in exchange for a low but guaranteed, level income for the rest of your life. However, the flat rates on these products are calculated on the assumption that you are as likely to climb Kilimanjaro at 95 as you are at 65, and we all know that isn't the case. The restrictions on these products can mean that if you don't live long into retirement, you family cannot benefit from what is left over.

Since George Osbourne introduced the Pension Freedom legislation, there is more flexibility than ever before; but with flexibility comes complexity. The decisions you make with your savings, investments and particularly your pension when you reach retirement make a massive difference to your life thereafter, so it is vital you make the right decisions to maximise your money and your life.

Having worked hard to save this money, making the right decisions at this stage will impact how you live the rest of your life, so it is vital you get it right. In order to address this, we created **The D.R.E.A.M. Income Strategy** to ensure that you maximise your hard-earned savings and turn them into a flexible dynamic income that can deliver what you want, when you want.

As an example, a few years ago a new client came to me when he was being forced to retire earlier than expected. He was 63, and it was too late in life to be going out and looking for another job doing what he did; plus, he hadn't planned to retire until he reached a specific financial milestone, and he needed another 2 years to get there. He was devastated, as he felt he had let his family down. He had promised his wife a new kitchen, regular trips abroad to see their children, and he felt he could no longer deliver on those promises.

Using the tools and systems in **The D.R.E.A.M. Income Strategy** we were able to show him how he could deliver on the retirement he had pledged. He could have everything he wanted, and more, just by making the right decisions around his money.

Business owners often want to retire gradually, so building an income that can be phased as your income reduces is essential to avoid paying too much tax. **The D.R.E.A.M. Income Strategy** can ensure you get the biggest bang for your buck, from those hard-earned savings.

### 5. Progress
Evolving with you, rather than stagnating!

If you get prepared in the right way, create a clear plan for the future, get your money growing faster with less risk, and create the right income for when you stop working, that will be great. However, will it still be right by this time next year? Probably not. There will be changes in your situation, the economy, legislation, the markets and the options available, which mean that you need to make changes to ensure your financial planning evolves with you, rather than gradually stagnating, as all too often is the case.

And this is the area where my former industry seriously falls down. Much of the financial services sector only wants to see you again if they think they can sell you something else. For those who do see you, generally they focus on the basic investment performance and nothing more. A proper review process needs to be so much more than that. It needs to look again into your financial future, new tax planning opportunities, how much you are spending/saving, as well as assessing the investments.

That's why, soon after I launched Efficient Portfolio in 2006, I developed **The Progressive Review Programme**. As a client, you want to have the peace of mind that your money is still working as hard for you as possible and is evolving and adapting to an ever-changing life.

This process was unique to us and was the reason many clients left their former Financial Adviser to join us. We delivered a review service like no other in ways that allowed us to do so much more to ensure our clients' financial planning actually evolved with them, rather than gradually grinding to a halt. As a pro tip, if you are thinking of using a Financial Adviser or Planner, ask them about their review process before you commit to using their services.

As a business owner, there is even more legislation to think about, and of course you have your business environment and trading conditions to think about too. This creates problems and opportunities, and so it is essential that your financial planning evolves within this ever-changing landscape.

### 6. Personal
It's about more than just the money!

I've been talking about money for a little while now, but I am sure you would agree that there is more to a happy financial future than just the money. In the brilliant book 'Thrive' by Arianna Huffington, founder of The Huffington Post, she talks about the 3 pillars of success.

Historically, people considered the keys to success were power and money, but what good does power and money do if you don't have wellbeing? If you don't have your health, and people around you who you love, then can you really be described as successful? When it comes to your financial future, the same applies. It is all very well focusing on the money side of retirement, but nobody really covers the 2 other key components: What you do with your time and how you maintain and even improve your wellbeing. You only have to turn on the TV to see a lot of rich, unhappy people.

That is why I wrote The Dream Retirement. I wanted to spread the message of what we did for our clients from a financial perspective, but I also wanted to be able to provide our former clients with much more than financial help. I wanted to be able to help them make the most of the time they have on this planet, and I wanted to help them improve their wellbeing, so that they could be as fulfilled as possible.

That is why we created **The Fulfilled Life Formula**. This was how we helped our clients do much more than just create a safe financial future. It was how we created a legacy, rather than just leaving material possessions in a Will. We did this with events, the book The Life Legacy Gift (which you can learn more about at **www.thetrusted.team/books/the-life-legacy-gift/** ) and by helping them build an Estate Plan, so that their money passed down through the generations in the manner they wanted, and with protection from divorce and Inheritance Tax. This made a massive difference to their future generations, or the causes that were closest to their hearts.

As an example, when you own your own business, you can usually leave that business to your children free of Inheritance Tax. Sounds good doesn't it? But let's think about what that means. Firstly, if something happens to you and your spouse during your children's younger years, they will inherit a lot of money the day the turn 18. Now that may lead to an amazing Fresher's Week, but probably not a good life thereafter. Whether they just waste it, lose it through marrying the son or daughter in law from hell, or worse, let it ruin their life, that probably isn't what you want. Also, once the business is sold, whether that be by your spouse or children, that money will now be liable to 40% Inheritance Tax when it passes down through the generation.

By using a Trust framework, you can ringfence that money to protect against these risks and allow your future generations to thrive. **The Fulfilled Life Formula** is how we did that for our clients.

I call these 6 steps to creating a better financial future, **The Efficient Money Method**.

## How Can We Help?

*"Someone's sitting in the shade today because someone planted a tree a long time ago."* Warren Buffet

There is obviously a lot to cover here, and I wanted to give you the basic stepping-stones to creating a better financial future, but this isn't the book to go into more detail. If, however, you would like to learn more about how financial planning can help you, why not book a call with us so that we can introduce you to one of our network of financial advisers? If you'd like to do this, please email **hello@efficientportfolio.co.uk**

Finally, earlier on in this chapter I promised to give you a way of taking a huge stride to a better financial future in just 4 minutes. In 2018 we developed '**The 2 Minute Retirement Plan'**- a mini financial plan that takes just 4 minutes to complete. This is completely free of charge and gives you an indication of what your future could look like. Take a huge step towards creating a better financial future for yourself, by visiting **www.efficientportfolio.co.uk/the-2-minute-retirement-plan/**

Remember, if you are failing to plan, you are planning to fail!

## Chapter Summary

- You need to ensure you get your business profits working as hard as possible, and allowing you to become financially free outside your company. You can do this by following 6 key steps, which we call 'The Efficient Money Method'.
- **Prepare**: Understand the psychology and systems that allow you to get to financial freedom as quickly as possible. Prepare, not repair.
- **Plan**: Have a clear vision of what your financial future looks like and understand the impact that decisions you make today will have on your future. If you're failing to plan, you're planning to fail!
- **Profit**: Get you money growing over and above inflation; working harder for you so you don't have to work for it! Get the best returns possible for a level of risk you are comfortable with!
- **Pension**: Once you reach financial freedom, you need to make the right decisions in order to create a dynamic income that will deliver the life you desire.
- **Progress**: Things change over time, and your finances are no different. You need to ensure that

your financial planning evolves with you, rather than stagnating over time.
- **Personal**: Life is about more than just the money. If you get it right, you can create an amazing lifestyle for you and the people you love. Create a legacy, not just a Will!

# Section 2: The Free Life Business M.O.D.E.L.

The 5-step guide to making more time in your business life.

| | |
|---|---|
| **M** | Magnify |
| **O** | Operations |
| **D** | Delegate |
| **E** | Energy |
| **L** | Life |

# Chapter 8: Magnify Your Moves

*"If everything's under control, you're not going fast enough."* Mario Andretti.

After having successfully propounded his famous theory of relativity, Albert Einstein would tour the various Universities in the United States, delivering lectures to a sea of bright-eyed students, eager to absorb his knowledge. On every lecture, he was always accompanied by his faithful chauffer, Harry, who would take a seat at the back of every auditorium they visited. One day, after Einstein had finished a lecture and was walking back to his car, Harry turned to him and said, "Professor Einstein, I've heard your lecture on relativity so many times, that if I were ever given the opportunity, I would be able to deliver it to perfection myself!"

"Very well," replied Einstein, "I'm going to Dartmouth next week. They don't know me there. You can deliver the lecture as Einstein, and I'll take your place as Harry!"

And Einstein delivered on his promise- the game was afoot. Upon arriving at Dartmouth, Harry presented himself as the great professor, whilst the famed scientist took a seat at the back of the auditorium. None the wiser to this private experiment, the students hung on Harry's every word, while he delivered the lecture to perfection and the real Einstein sat in the back row playing 'chauffer'.

However, there was a sudden plot twist that threatened to expose the rouse. Just as Harry was descending from the podium, one of the research assistants intercepted him, and

began to ask him a question on the theory of relativity....
one that involved a lot of complex calculations and
equations. This was not normal territory for the talk, so
Harry had to think on his feet. Harry thought for a moment,
and then replied to the assistant "The answer to this
question is very simple! In fact, it's so simple, that I'm going
to let my chauffer answer it!"

If you want to create a better work life balance, then you
need to work out ways to magnify the work you do. If you
can complete one piece of work, but allow many people to
benefit from it, two amazing things happen. Firstly, you can
make more money in less time. Secondly, and perhaps more
importantly, you can help more people than you would
have been able to previously, and potentially they can pay
less for that help too. Everyone is happy. The question is,
how can you do this?

## One to Many

*"Why are you trying to fit in, when you were born to stand out."* Andy Harrington

Many businesses, like my own financial planning firm once
did, involve spending a lot of time with clients on a '1 to 1'
basis. The traditional model is to go out and try and meet
lots of new clients, spend your time with those potential
clients whilst you try to show them the value of your
service, and then hope to continue to see them regularly in
order to try to provide them with an ongoing service. All
this involves a lot of time, and, as I have already talked
about earlier in this book, we only have so much time to
work with. So how can you achieve more in less time?

One of the best ways is to identify how you can change your business from a '1 to 1' business, to a '1 to many' business. How can you pitch to many potential clients at once? How can you service many clients at the same time? Let me give you a few examples, initially of my former business, but of some others too.

At Efficient Portfolio we wanted to educate people about their money, because by knowing and understanding more, they were more inclined to act to improve their financial future. As a result, one of our marketing approaches was 'The Wealth Workshop', which I mentioned earlier. Back then, and more acutely today with The Trusted Team, through public speaking I can build trust, educate and then essentially pitch our proposition to many people all at once. With Efficient Portfolio, by taking the '1 to many' approach, in one day I could generate enough new clients for several of our advisers, as well as giving a better financial education to those people who needed it.

One of the biggest problems the financial services industry has is the ongoing servicing of existing clients. Much of the industry still works on the basis that the adviser only wants to see you if they think they can sell you something new, not to service what you already have. Part of the reason for this is because otherwise, over time, they get bogged down with seeing existing clients, and they have no time to see new clients, which is where they make more of their money from.

As a result, you either get the advisers who don't want to provide ongoing service at all, so they can see plenty of new clients, or you get advisers who cap the number of clients that they look after and see no one new. Neither are ideal situations.

When I set up Efficient Portfolio, I was determined to provide a good ongoing service to our clients. Initially having a good support team around me was enough, but after a while I realised there still needed to be more innovation. As a result, we introduced 'The Client Review Workshop'. We split the review into two elements: The client specific content, like the changes happening in their life; and the aspects that applied to most clients, like investment performance, planning opportunities, legislation changes and some more interesting things like your 'bucket list'. All of the elements that applied to most people, were covered in The Client Review Workshop, to a room full of clients. This gave us more time to cover generic issues in a cohesive fashion and ensure that the private meetings were far more focussed and meaningful. I also spent far less time conducting reviews but achieved better results and client satisfaction.

By introducing 'The Wealth Workshop' and 'The Client Review Workshop, I massively increased the number of people I could help, thus making the business more profitable and my clients more confident, educated and, ultimately, feeling more secure about their futures. It may not have always gone perfectly, and in some cases it may not always have been as good as seeing someone 1 to 1, but the significant increase in what we could achieve, motivated me to continue to innovate and make the process even better than 1 to 1 over time. That was certainly my experience.

Let's look at another person who has transformed their business by employing the '1 to many' approach, to show that the method translates to other sectors.

James Dewane had been in the electrical industry for just over 25 years, having served his apprenticeship in a small family firm in Ireland. Whilst he had a great career as an electrician it was not without its ups and downs. In 2007 he had a thriving company, nine staff, three vans, a car and a shop front – only to find himself on the brink of personal bankruptcy because two developers he was working with went out of business owing him a lot of money. Although he appeared to have a great turnover, the business was not profitable, so he could not recover from the failure. He had no choice but to start again.

He threw himself into learning how to market direct to the consumer by taking courses and reading books, and he managed to create a brand-new business within the domestic sector; however, he was still exchanging time for money, and there was only so much time in the week. He decided to rethink his approach. He decided to help other electricians market their business, using all the tools he had learned. He downed tools and started speaking at events where his audience were 'the competition'. He wrote a book, which you can download for free at **http://www.jdewane.com/** and he created a membership site that delivered marketing courses to his clients, long after he had left them. He has used the '1 to many' approach to create a far more profitable, less time intensive business, that ultimately means he reaches a much wider audience.

James and I are not the only ones that have done this to boost our work life balance, and to deliver to more people in less time. Whether it is delivering services through video, websites, seminars, or workshops, you need to think about how you can reposition your service to achieve more in less time. If you ever want to get better at something, find the best coach you can, and then totally immerse yourself in their work. If you do that, you will make such huge strides forward in short spaces of time, it will have a massive impact on your business and life.

## The Framework Formula

Throughout my coaching journey, one of most important things that I have learnt is that if you want your teaching to be memorable and impactful, you need to create a system. It is no good trying to teach people the 101 things they need to know about your sector to be successful, you need to break it down into manageable chunks. If I ask you to remember those 101 things, you have no chance, but if I ask you to remember 6 systems, you have a much better chance. Within each of those systems, you can then remember the steps needed.

**The Better Future Framework (BFF)** is an example. So is The Efficient Money Method that I taught at The Wealth Workshop. By breaking it down into bite size chunks it makes it easier for the audience to remember and understand, whether you are delivering it through video, the web or in person. It doesn't just benefit the receiver; it also benefits you in many ways too.

A well-thought-out framework will force you to refine your thoughts and pick out the most important elements. It will ensure you package the most relevant pieces together. It will mean that you have built your own unique intellectual product, something that no other business can offer, differentiating you from your competitors on a factor other than price. This last point is really important if what you do differently to your competitors comes down to price alone; there will always be someone who will do it cheaper, so the price will continue to fall.

Creating your own framework gives you a unique product that no one else can complete with on a like for like basis. Not only that, but it is intellectual property like this that makes your business more valuable. Finally, when it comes to presenting the content, the system makes what you do a lot more memorable. As a result, you will be able to present without notes- one of the keys to becoming successful speaker.

There are lots of aspects to creating your own framework, and, to do it justice, you need to dedicate some focussed time and be prepared to refine, and refine time and time again; however, here is my quick-fire approach to creating a memorable framework.

1. List all of the most important areas of what you do.
2. Ideally using a mind mapping software (I like iMindMap) group them into areas. No fewer than 3, no more than 8.
3. For each of these steps, identify the pain you are trying to remove for people, the area where you help them. For example, with regards to creating financial freedom, we helped people Prepare, Plan, create Profit, create a Pension, Progress, and also help with the Personal side of their finances too.

You'll notice that all steps of my framework begin with the letter 'P'; alliteration or acronyms are not essential, but they make your framework punchier and more memorable.

4. Split each step into stages (i.e. their component parts) and name each of these areas. If you want to employ the literary techniques I've mentioned, an online thesaurus is a great help. Alliteration and acronyms will make the stages of your framework easier for you and your audience to remember and make them more phonetically pleasing.
5. Design a graphic that illustrates these areas. Here is The Efficient Money Method as an example.

## Stories

*"Marketing is no longer about the stuff that you make, but about the stories you tell."* - Seth Godin

In 'The Dream Retirement', I talk about the work of economist **Josef Zweimuller** of the University of Zurich, who co-authored a study that found that early retirement, as much as we may crave it, seems to be bad for our health.

"[A]MONG BLUE-COLLAR WORKERS, WE SEE THAT WORKERS WHO RETIRE EARLIER HAVE A HIGHER MORTALITY RATE AND THESE EFFECTS ARE PRETTY LARGE."

He drew this conclusion from assessing two very similar sets of blue-collar workers in Austria where a change in the unemployment insurance system presented a unique opportunity for the study. This policy change allowed older workers in eligible regions to retire up to 3.5 years earlier than comparable workers in non-eligible regions. The programme generated substantial variation in the actual retirement age, which, arguably, was driven only by financial incentives and not driven by differences in individuals' health status. This let them examine the causal impact of early retirement on mortality.

The study showed that for every extra year of early retirement, workers lost about two months of life expectancy. This is not the first study to show a strong relationship between early retirement and earlier death so we can draw the conclusion that we aren't actually very good at retirement. The old saying of 'working yourself into an early grave' should perhaps be revised.

I found this fascinating, as whilst we crave stopping work early, it is actually bad for us! I suppose, in retirement, every day is a Saturday, so there is no reason not to have that extra glass or wine, that pizza for tea, or have that lie in.

I use this story to introduce why I wrote 'The Dream Retirement'. I used it in the book, and I have used it in radio interviews since. Every time I find an interesting story with an interesting angle or link to an aspect of what I do, I add it to my story database. That way, every time I talk or write about that subject, I can introduce it with a 'sticky story', as the authors Chip & Dan Heath talk about in their book 'Made to Stick'. A 'sticky story' literally 'sticks' with the audience and holds resonance with them.

In fact, if you also read Carmine Gallo's 'Talk Like TED'- an excellent look into what makes the most successful TED talks so 'sticky'- it is all about the stories. Each TED talk lasts

18 minutes, and generally the best format for this time is splitting it into 3 stories, each with a learning outcome.

Having a database of stories is a really powerful thing. When you get the opportunity to speak, explain a key concept, write a blog or record a video, you can make it more impactful with a 'sticky story'.

The most important story of all is your own. The one that makes you the expert. When Andy Harrington talks about it, he refers to is as your 'Expert Positioning Story'. If I am given the opportunity to talk to an unfamiliar audience, in most instances I need to explain who I am, and why they should listen to me. If I don't, they will have a lot of unanswered questions, and they will also question why they should respect my opinion. You should therefore always be armed with a compelling 'Expert Positioning Story', for whenever the need arises.

You might even have different variations of this story, for different audiences. At the start of this book I told you a few of my Expert Positioning Stories: The meeting with Uncle Bill, The Dickens Process at Unleash the Power Within, and having 'The Dream Retirement' published. I could have provided a timeline of what I'd done throughout my career, but it would have been really dull. Making it into a story, a story with 3 distinct chapters, makes it much more interesting for the reader. Even more so when you are presenting. I have lost track of how many times I've seen people stand on stage with a power point slide listing out their career history and a CV of their experience or qualifications. A story makes it far more for interesting, it creates more emotion and, as a result, it makes it more memorable. It takes the reader or listener on a journey.

Stories are one of the oldest mediums in the world. Before we had YouTube, blogs or even books, we passed on our wisdom from one generation to another using stories. Sitting around the campfire, these stories were there to provide a learning lesson. And this tradition hasn't changed: My parents telling the story of 'The Boy Who Cried Wolf' was one of the best pieces of advice my parents gave me!

For your Expert Positioning Story, you will need structure. You need to identify which of your key stories can be combined to make one longer and more impactful narrative. Work on it.

In my Better Future Framework, I get people to do 'The Story Playbook' exercise to help them build their own expert story. You can find out more about this at **www.thetrusted.team/BFF**.

When you get the chance to tell your story, it is often an excellent business opportunity, so have it planned, practiced and polished! 'Prior preparation prevents poor performance'!

## Do It Once, Use It Many Times!

The reason for building a good directory of stories is so that you can reuse the same material time and time again. You can massively magnify your business success by using the 'Do it Once, Use it Many Times' approach.

When Caryl and I first got together, I must have been a lot more romantic than I am now, because after just 6 weeks of dating, I whisked her away to Venice for her birthday. We had a wonderful few days walking the streets of the spectacular city, exploring the likes of the Ponte di Rialto, Basilica di San Marco and all the magnificent markets, shops, buildings and restaurants you can find by aimlessly wandering the labyrinth of side streets.

Because of this trip, we said we would go back to Venice for our 10$^{th}$ anniversary. We tried to refamiliarise ourselves with the map to try and work out where we had been; we tried to find the best restaurants online and tried to speak to friends who we knew had been there. As a result of all this research, we had a wonderful trip back to Venice in January 2016- a magical time to experience this city as it isn't overrun with tourists. We almost had a personal tour of Basilica di San Marco, as opposed to queuing for hours to even get onto the group tour. We walked straight up the Campanile di San Marco, as opposed to queuing for hours for that too. It is a enchanting place, and in 4 days we got to do and see a lot, as well as eat in some of the best restaurants.

My point here is that, had I written up just a little of our experiences the first time around, it would have been much easier to track down some of the things we wanted to revisit. In addition, over the years that past since our first visit, we would have been able to help others visiting Venice to really enjoy their experience to the full.

Following on from our second visit, I knew at least two other couples who were going to be heading to Venice for a similar visit, and I knew they were going to ask us for recommendations. As a result, what I should have done the first time, but did do the second time, was write up a list of top tips for Venice. It didn't take long, and it ensures that if we go back again for our 20th wedding anniversary, we can remember what we did, where we stayed and where we ate from our previous visit. Not only that, but I can share that with the 2 couples that went soon afterwards, and also any who subsequently decide to go. That write up then featured in our blog and in our newsletter. What has been done once, can be used many times. The impact it then has is far greater for the same amount of effort.

There are lots of ways you can do this in your business. If you record a video, as well as using it as one video, can you break it down into chunks to make it into smaller videos too. You could transcribe that video into text and turn it into a blog article, something for your newsletter, or for your website. You could extract the audio and turn it into a podcast. You could use the text from this video and add it to the text of other videos to make your next book, and you could then turn that into an audiobook or even an online course. One video will create masses of content if you choose to recycle it in different ways. You could even hire someone to follow you around, and document what you talk about, and turn that into content. And with the rise in AI, doing all of this could not be easier. All of this is content without it costing you any time at all, which as we know, is our more valuable resource!

If you write a piece of text for a client, maybe in an email or in a report, that can become the basis of a blog article or newsletter. Or perhaps an advertorial in the local magazine? Every piece of content that gets produced by you and your business should have you thinking, 'how can we use this again and again?'

Another brilliant way I did this at Efficient Portfolio was something called the 'Blair Bible', which helped our advisers a tremendous amount. It got its name from a story that former leader of the Conservative Party William Hague tells.

As leader of the opposition, being stood across the house of commons from Tony Blair, Hague got the opportunity to witness a master debater. Blair was known to have the world at his fingertips, in what was referred to as the Blair Bible. If Hague had a rant about Labour policy on oil, Blair would immediately flick to 'O' in The Blair Bible, look down to 'Oil', and then list a number of facts about how Labour had improved the oil situation, and the Conservatives had damaged it. As a result of the Blair Bible, he could instantly counter the arguments that Hague, or anyone else for that matter, threw at him.

Over time, the way that Hague learnt to counter act the effectiveness of the Blair Bible was to only reveal the subject of each question or statement in the last few words. As a result, he would have Blair frantically flicking through

The Blair Bible in order to try and identify the facts that were going to form the basis of his counter argument.

In our business, we had to simplify complicated financial concepts to our clients. One of the most effective ways we did this was with pictures. Back in the days of my early financial planning career, I was shown numerous sketches that explained different financial concepts. And these images proved invaluable later in my career.

A few years ago, when I used to see huge amounts of clients, I would find myself drawing the same sketches to explain estate planning, how a wrap account works or how a pension can be drawn down several times in the same day. It occurred to me that I should build a PowerPoint slide that would do the same thing. I am certainly no artist, so a professionally laid out slide ensured that the clients got the best understanding of the concept every time. It also meant that I didn't miss anything either, and it saved me time by not having to draw the same sketch time and again.

I initially built the Blair Bible for my benefit when sitting with clients. I then started to use the same slides in my presentations to accountants and solicitors as part of my Trusted Team presentation. Then again in seminars like 'The Wealth Workshop' and 'The Dream Retirement Dinner'. Then it got even better as I employed other advisers who I could show the same slides to for their training and use. This also ensured that the advisers could professionally explain concepts to clients in the same way as I do, hence creating consistency, continuity and maintaining compliance. These became so effective that we created Outstanding Operations videos, but more on that in the next chapter. The Blair Bible was the ultimate example of doing something once and using it many times.

Building a database of stories is the same thing. Speaking to many people rather than to one person is making you work 1 to many. Create web-based content that people can consume time and again, and you are at it again.

Look at the expertise you have, and what you do on a day-to-day basis, and work out how you could do it once, to magnify the results you get from your efforts. The Story Playbook tool I've already mentioned is a great starting point, so if you'd like a free copy, please get in touch. Alternatively, you may benefit more from a free coaching call with me. In either case, please email us on **hello@thetrusted.team** to learn more.

## The Story of Peloton

Personal fitness is big business. Ever since the early 20th century, the appetite to employ a personal trainer or coach has been ravenous, especially during the 1970s and 1980s, when 'PTs' exploded onto the health scene in shock of technicolour lycra and insatiable enthusiasm.

Having your very own personal trainer, who worked with you on a one-to-one basis and developed a personalised fitness plan just for you, was seen as the pinnacle of social status. Moreover, personal training became regarded as the ultimate, if not only, way to achieve optimum health and an enviable physique.

And there were, and certainly still are, huge benefits to using a personal trainer. Clients received tailored programs for their specific needs, as well as direct guidance during workouts to ensure proper form, technique and the best possible results. There was also the added perk of being accountable to someone, who directly motivated you and gave you their undivided attention to help you reach your goals.

For personal trainers, the demand for their services meant that their careers skyrocketed. Clients couldn't get enough of them, and their diaries were bursting at the seams. But in this sweet spot of high demand and relentless workloads, the cracks started to appear.

Working on a one-to-one basis meant that time was the enemy. For personal trainers, there was no time to take on more clients and continue to grow their businesses. They simply didn't have the capacity to help more people. So, they started charging more and offering fewer, shorter, less convenient workout sessions in a bid to make more money and see more clients. You don't need me to tell you that this was not a popular move!

With the personal training market becoming increasingly expensive and elitist, and clients becoming irked at the lack of time slots available that didn't fit with their own busy schedules, the personal fitness craze was suddenly facing crisis. There was still a demand for fitness and health, but consumers couldn't afford to pay increasing fees for a service that didn't fit in with their busy lifestyles.

It was at this point that Peloton side-swiped the industry and changed the personal fitness race.

Peloton realised that the one-to-one personal training model was significantly flawed. For a fitness business to continue to flourish in the modern world, it needed to be scalable and adopt a one-to-many approach. Even more than that, the product or service needs to be accessible at any time of day, in any country in the world. It also needs to be more affordable and encourage a subscription-based model that has no limitations on numbers of users.

So, in 2012, Peloton revolutionised the fitness industry by introducing a technology driven approach to personalised fitness instruction. They achieved this by combining high-quality exercise equipment with live and on-demand streaming classes, allowing thousands of users to participate in group workouts from home, at a time that is convenient for them; whether that's at 5am, late in the evening, or in between Zoom meetings when they're working from home.

Peloton's revolutionary approach addressed the common barriers to traditional fitness models, such as time constraints, gym accessibility, and costs. By scaling personalised instruction to a large audience, Peloton has made expert-led workouts more accessible and engaging for a broader demographic, disrupting the traditional personal training paradigm and inspiring numerous competitors in the connected fitness space.

Accessible fitness options like group classes, online programs, and fitness apps have seen an astronomical rise in the last 10 years, as people demand more flexibility and convenience, access to real-time metrics and data, and a sense of community in a virtual world.

So, what can we learn from the likes of Peloton? In service-based businesses, the traditional one-on-one client approach often limits your reach and your impact in so many ways. Imagine if you could amplify your expertise—helping not just one but many clients simultaneously, all within the same amount of time it takes to assist a single client?

In business, taking a one-to-many approach, instead of a one-to-one approach can transform how you accelerate your business. Whether that means taking your marketing from networking to social media, educating your prospect from discussion to online course, or servicing your clients from annual review meetings to group workshops and webinars, if you want to scale while working less, ask yourself, 'how can I change my one-to-one, into roles one-to-many, so I can help many people in the time it took me to help just one previously?'

This is why I created the 'Magnification Mastery' for my Trusted Team members. This powerful strategy transforms your one-on-one services into scalable, one-to-many solutions. By doing so, you multiply your impact, helping more people in less time. I believe that this is the ultimate way to unlock your potential, extend your reach and elevate your business to new heights. Just one part of this strategy alone reduced the time it took to service all our clients at Efficient Portfolio by 50%, whilst increasing the value they received and also generating more fees.

If you would like to find out more about how you can use this revolutionising tool in your business, we'd love to explain more on our Discovery Call, so please get in touch by emailing **hello@thetrusted.team**

## Chapter Summary

- Help more people in less time by identifying ways that you can deliver what you do to many people at once, rather than just one to one. Whether that is through digital marketing or public speaking, leverage what you do with your time.
- Give people a clear message of what you do by creating a Unique Business System- a system full of your intellectual property so that you can easily share it through a variety of different mediums.
- Get more traction with your message by identifying stories that help you more easily explain each in a more memorable way. As a business, use them time and again.
- Make an impact and build trust with your audience by building an Expert Positioning Story so that every time you need to explain where you have come from, and why your audience should trust you, you have a polished message that portrays what you need it to.
- Achieve more by building everything with a view to using it many times.
- Use the Magnification Mastery to take your business from a one-to-one approach to a one-to-many model to save time and grow your business.

# Chapter 9: Outstanding Operations

*"Most people spend more time and energy going around problems than trying to solve them."* Henry Ford

I once read about a new Managing Director of a world-famous sweet factory. After years of success, the company's profits had been gradually slipping, and the new MD was brought in to re-energise the business. His first action was to look at the recipe involved in making the world-famous sweets, and he saw that there are 40 different ingredients. This seemed like a huge list of ingredients for such a tiny product, so he asked the confectioners to make a number of different versions of the sweet, and in each one to drop one ingredient.

After trying all the versions, the new MD identified the version that had no marked impact on the flavour and set about making the new recipe with the one less ingredient. The company immediately reduced its costs, increased its efficiencies and, after only a couple of months, the benefit to the company's bottom line was evident. The MD calls his confectioners in again and asks them to repeat the exercise. Again, the variation with one less ingredient but no noticeable impact to the flavour is selected, and the recipe readapted again. Sure enough, the benefits to the bottom line are seen just a few short months later. So, he repeats the exercise again, and again, until the recipe is just thirty ingredients, and at its most profitable.

This seems like a powerful formula for success: Give the customers the same experience whilst reducing costs each time, which should mean that you increase your profits. However, a year on from the changes, the company started to see sales falling. The now-well-established and highly praised MD cannot fathom why this is happening. At each stage there has been no marked change in the flavour, but people are now buying fewer of their sweets. Why would this be? Whilst the MD is deliberating, he opens a pack of the original sweets, those that were produced before any changes were made. He pops one in his mouth and is blown away by its flavour. He pops one of his new simplified sweets into his mouth and is amazed at the lack of flavour. How has this happened? There was no noticeable difference at each stage, but the compounded effect of these changes has made a huge impact.

And therein lies the problem. In business, we often come up with great ideas, but as that idea is handed from one employee to the next the message gradually gets lost or forgotten. In business it is often easy to find great ideas that work, but over time we stop doing them. Usually not intentionally, but perhaps because of a of staff change, or perhaps because you get too busy. Overtime, what was once a brilliant piece of work loses its sparkle. Just like the sweets, over the shorter timeframes there is no noticeable difference, but when compounded over a longer timeframe, the difference is huge.

If you want to run an outstanding organisation, you need to create outstanding operations. Outstanding operations are created by having clear documents and continually evolving processes.

One of the most impactful business books I have ever read was 'The E-Myth Revisited: Why Most Small Businesses Fail' by Michael Gerber. I had the good fortune to be introduced to this book around the time I was setting up Efficient

Portfolio; ironically by someone who ran the large IFA firm I was working under in London.

I remember reading that book and starting to understand that a business owner needed an 'entrepreneur', a 'manager' and a 'technician'. We all have elements of each in us, but we will always feel a strong bias to one of those areas. Identifying at an early stage what I was, and what I wasn't, was a powerful learning point. Later, at Tony Robbins' Business Mastery he talked about it in similar terms but instead describing 'the technician' as 'the artist'.

The E-Myth is a brilliant book for many reasons, but for me there was one epiphany moment. I knew I needed to employ someone if I was to truly progress, but what I couldn't get my head around was how I took what was in my head and got someone else to do it.

Michael Gerber helped me see through that. What he preaches in 'The E-Myth' is that to delegate a process, you first need to do that role yourself. You master that role, identify the way you want it done, and then you document the process. That way you can then assign the job to someone else, ideally someone who is actually going to be better at it than you. Simple but genius at the same time.

## Clone Yourself
*"The more I practice, the luckier I get."* Jerry Barber

In the words of a solicitor I know, 'to really allow the business to grow, you need to clone yourself.' This is achieved by creating outstanding operations or processes, which deliver repeatable service from anyone in your business.

My initial problem when I employed Sainabou, my first employee, was to work out how I got across to her all the things that needed doing to build a client's plan following the initial meeting. I looked at 'The E-Myth's' message, and I created a document called 'Meeting Follow Up.' It certainly wasn't rocket science, but that document evolved over the years, into something we still used with every new client until we sold the business.

When I initially read 'The E-Myth', I thought that the magic was in me creating my own processes, and people following them. How wrong I was. The magic is what happens after you delegate those processes. If you get it right, you'll end up delegating the role to someone who is better at that role. That was the key to the success of so many amazing entrepreneurs, including Steve Jobs, Henry Ford and Richard Branson, however it is the latter who is probably best known for it.

In the words or Richard Branson, 'People are a company's biggest asset, and in order for a business to survive and grow, a leader must learn to delegate duties effectively. I learned very early in my career that one of the smartest things a leader can do is hire people who excel in areas they are weaker in.'

Overtime, the people you delegate to will continue to improve how the process is completed. It's pivotal that you ask them to continually update the documented process, so that over the course of time, they turn your operations manual into 'Outstanding Operations'.

This all sounds brilliant, but do you really need to bother with documenting it all? Isn't that just more work? It is more work, but it is some of the most valuable work that you will ever do. When someone is off sick, leaves the company, or is promoted, it is this document that keeps the process happening. When we take on a new member of staff, or move an employee to a new role, one of the first thing we do is ask them to read the relevant section of this document. It ensures they can get up to speed in their role much more quickly and far more effectively.

Let me give you an example of an evolving process. When Caryl and I first got together, and I was starting to get to know her family better, we realised we had different eating habits. Caryl's family were from the mining community in Wales and my family from the farming community in Rutland, so there were some distinct differences. One was the way we liked our beef cooked. As farmers, we wanted the plate to still be mooing; Juicy, pink beef with blood dripping off the plate. Whereas the Blandford's wanted all signs of blood gone; they wanted their beef well done.

One way of solving this problem was to give Caryl the end piece of the joint, as that was better done than the middle, but here we encountered another problem. In theory, this should have worked quite well as Caryl quite liked that rough end of the joint of meat, but it didn't. If we ate at my parents' house, my mum would always cut the end off the joint and discard it before she roasted it. There was of course a new end bit, but it wasn't the same as the natural rough end to the joint.

Some investigation was needed, so I asked my mum why she always did this. "Charles," she replied, "that's part of the recipe. It is what my mum taught me, so that is why we always do it."

That's not good enough, I thought. "I need to speak to Nanna." So off I went to ask Nanna. "Nanna, why do you always cut the end off the piece of beef? Caryl likes that bit, but Mum says it's part of the recipe, and I don't see why!"

"Charles" she replied, "that is simple. We cut the end of the joint of beef off because otherwise it doesn't fit into my roasting tin, and if I don't use that tin, it won't fit into my oven!"

Just because something has always been done in a particular way, doesn't mean it should continue to be done that way. The process of delegating will allow you to find even more efficient ways to complete that role, because rather than just doing it as you have always done, it forces you to think about the best way to do that specific role.

Having 'The Outstanding Operations Manual' will ensure your business delivers more predictable results to your clients and it will ensure that your business is more secure in the event of something unexpected happening to you or one of your team. In addition to this, it will make your business more valuable. The Intellectual Property (IP) that is contained within that document is what makes you unique. Someone buying that business can see how that can be continued after you have left, if it is clearly documented.

So, ensure you have a clearly documented Outstanding Operations Manual for everything that happens in your business and make sure that the documented processes are revisited regularly so that they evolve with your business. When someone new joins your business, make sure they use that document as their guide and as the basis for their training and note taking, and ask them to add any missing areas as they go. That way, all the things they learn in their first few weeks that have been missed from the Manual will be added for future employees.

All this might sound like a lot of work, but it doesn't need to be. Here are some top tips on how you can massively increase the effectiveness of your 'Outstanding Operations Manual' without it taking you an eternity to create.

- Make the process visual: A simple flow diagram from Microsoft Word SmartArt makes for a really easy to follow visual process.
- Film your work: Use tools like CamStudio, Zoom or Camtasia to record your screen and your commentary. That way, you can build an Outstanding Operation whilst working on the job. All you need to do is to add a running commentary to what you are doing. When you are training a new employee, record that.
- Borrow and reference external content: Find videos and articles online that explain a concept and drop those links into your OOM too.
- Start by asking yourself what your core business areas are. These should be the most important steps of your client journey and the most important things you do behind the scenes. At the same time as you write up each Outstanding Operation, identify what one improvement you like to make to each that would make it run even more efficiently.

By creating your Outstanding Operation for each of these areas, and incorporating the one improvement you wanted to make for each, you can produce a massively powerful document in very little time. As they say, 'hard work never killed anyone, but why take the risk!' In my Better Future Framework, I get people to do an exercise to help them identify the areas of their business that need an Outstanding Operation building. You can find out more about this at **www.thetrusted.team/BFF**.

## Phenomenal Process

The other way to clone yourself is to have, what I would call, a Phenomenal Process that you lead your clients through. In the last chapter we looked at building a Framework Formula, which is all of your intellectual property put into a manageable process, so that you can teach and explain it easily. This is great for explaining the underlying concepts of what you do, but it doesn't explain how you actually do it.

Back in 2019, I had the pleasure of meeting 3 new local marketing agencies to help build our strategy. I love talking about marketing, as you might have gathered from parts of this book, and meeting three different agencies allowed us to listen to variety of ideas and find the best fit company for our needs. They all met with us for an initial meeting, which was great; we chatted about our business, and what we wanted our marketing to look like, and where they saw the opportunities.

Throughout all of the first meetings, I found myself wondering, what is the next step? If I work with them, what does it look like in practical terms? It is fantastic to talk about marketing concepts, but as a business owner, I need to know what is involved. How much time, how many meetings, timeframes, etc. Not one of them explained to me their process, and in every case, I found myself asking what it would actually look like.

Maybe this was a reflection of speaking to more 'creative types', but I'd say it equally applies to both left-brain thinkers and the right-brain thinkers. I can't remember ever having a clearly laid out explanation of the process from any accountants or solicitors I have met either.

As a business owner, the steps of your process are obvious to you. You know your subject like the back of your hand, and you assume that everyone else does too. The reality is that no one else does. Even people who have used similar services won't know exactly how you will work with them, and people who are using your industry's services for the first time don't stand a chance.

When I first joined the crazy commission hungry world of City Financial Partners and Biggsy back in 1999, I was told that there was a simple 2-step sales process: Book the client in for what was imaginatively know as a 'first', which was a fact-finding meeting, where you needed to find out what you could sell them; and then to book the equally imaginatively named 'second', which was the sales meeting in proper. Pretty straight forward. I knew what is was, but the clients didn't.

Over the years of constantly evolving Efficient Portfolio's business practices, we improved what we did, we embraced financial planning as opposed to just giving financial advice and therefore added additional steps to improve the structure.

Our process used to look like this:

**Free Finance Call**

A free call with a Financial Planner to make sure we could help, and to identify the best person at Efficient Portfolio to do so.

**The Exploration Meeting**

A face-to-face meeting with a Financial Planner to help people understand how we worked, understand where they currently were with their finances and, most importantly, to help us give them a clearer understanding of what they wanted to achieve in the future. This meeting was free of charge.

**The Efficient Financial Plan**

A bespoke financial plan that gave clients clarity on whether they were on track for the financial future they wanted. This document analysed their existing financial planning to work out what was good and what was not, and it then gave the client the approach and strategies to improve; ultimately improving that financial future. This included strategies for investments, for retirement, including pensions, an estate plan, so that clients could protect their assets for their loved ones, and other elements of financial planning too. We sent this in the post and electronically and charged a flat fee for the plan, but it was covered by a 100% money back guarantee.

**The Planning Meeting**

Once clients had had the chance to read their Efficient Financial Plan, they then had a Planning Meeting with their Financial Planner. If they had any questions, this meeting ensured they were answered, and that they understood everything clearly, so they could make the best decisions to move forward. The fees for implementing our ideas were all clearly laid out in the plan.

**The Implementation Meeting**

An opportunity for the Client Relationship Manager to guide people through paperwork to implement clients' financial plans in the most pain free and efficient way.

**The Progressive Review Programme**

An ongoing review service that ensured clients kept on top of their finances, and continued to make the most of the financial planning opportunities that presented themselves, because you need to ensure your planning evolves with your ever-changing life, the legislation and the investment markets. This included face to face meetings with their Financial Planner, workshops and regular updates.

This process was called 'The Efficient Wealth Management Process' and was clearly explained to all new clients before and during our Exploration Meeting. As a result, our clients clearly knew what the process looked like.

As another example, at The Trusted Team, we help you grow both your business and time off with the following Phenomenal Client Process:

**Trusted Team Workshops**: Building strong partnerships and gaining accountability are crucial for the success of any business. That's why our Trusted Team Workshops are so important. Every two months, whether live in person or virtual, you and your business can benefit from these interactive sessions. These workshops not only provide coaching to enhance your business strategies but also feature special guest speakers who expand your knowledge on a wide range of specialist topics. You'll leave each workshop equipped with immediately implementable strategies and tools, while also expanding your professional network, setting your business up for greater success.

**Business Growth Online Accelerator**: Imagine propelling your business forward without sacrificing your precious time. The Business Growth Online Accelerator delivers expert digital coaching right to your fingertips, empowering you to learn and implement growth strategies at your own pace. It helps you to unlock sustainable success, boost your bottom line, and navigate market changes with confidence—all while maintaining control of your busy schedule.

**Trusted Learning Lunches**: Nourish your mind while you feed your body with Trusted Learning Lunches! Time is a precious commodity for business owners, but learning and growth and still fundamental to your success. That's why we deliver quick-fire learning at a time when you are likely to have some downtime. Our monthly live sessions serve up a diverse menu of topics, from business strategies to cutting-edge subjects like AI and longevity. In just one lunch break, gain insights that fuel your professional growth and personal development, keeping you ahead in an ever-evolving world.

**The Kaizen Constant**: In today's competitive landscape, continuous improvement is crucial for business success. The Kaizen (改善) Constant, inspired by Toyota's growth strategy, offers your team a monthly live meeting to collaboratively enhance your business. Save time on meeting preparation, gain fresh perspectives from peers, and cultivate a culture of ongoing refinement—all key to staying ahead in your industry.

**The Trusted Team Socials**: Building strong connections fosters trust, opens new opportunities, and creates a supportive network essential for business growth, collaboration, and long-term success in today's interconnected world. You can do all of that with the Trusted Team Socials. From wine tastings to golf outings, these diverse events blend business with pleasure, creating an atmosphere where partnerships flourish naturally. Strengthen your professional network, discover potential collaborations, and enjoy memorable experiences—all while laying the groundwork for future business success in a relaxed, engaging environment.

**The Mastermind Maximiser**: In business, having a support network and staying accountable are crucial for sustained success. The Mastermind Maximiser offers bi-monthly sessions where you can tap into the collective wisdom of your peers, share triumphs, and address challenges head-on. This powerful forum strengthens your connections, keeps you focused on your goals, and provides timely solutions—ensuring you stay on track for growth and excellence.

When you add all these elements together, you cannot help but to grow, improve your work life balance and enjoy life more!

By building a Phenomenal Process, you can clearly explain what each client can expect. In addition, you are making the process repeatable, which means you can over time clone yourself and get other people do the same thing. Our clients were told that, regardless of the adviser they saw, they would all follow the same process.

As the face of the business, I used to think that people only wanted to see me. Over time, I realised that wasn't the case. If people knew that they would be guided through the same process regardless of the Financial Planner, they were happy that they were still getting my expertise, even without me seeing them. In addition, clients also got the same advice, as we managed decisions like investment strategy from the top down.

Finally, through our Outstanding Operations, specifically through my recording of what the ideal Exploration Meeting and Planning Meeting looked and felt like, and by using documents like The Blair Bible, my Financial Planners even sounded like me! I wanted them to, because I wanted them to reach the same level I had in a fraction of that time.

With regards to your Phenomenal Process, it is important that you name each stage. The reason to name them is so that they are unique to you. You could not get an Efficient Financial Plan from anywhere else than from Efficient Portfolio. It differentiates you from your competitors and means that you can't got through The Efficient Wealth Management Process of the Better Future Framework, for example, with anyone other than us.

Make sure when you name your process, and the stages within it, the names are based on the benefits people get from using them. Focus on the benefits not the features. As Dan Sullivan says "he who names it, owns it".

In order that you can get your time back, you need to clone yourself with repeatable and scalable processes, so I have put together an exercise for you to work through. This can be found in The Entrepreneurial Happiness Workbook, that you can download for free from **www.thetrusted.team/books/entrepreneurial-happiness**.

## Chapter Summary

- Make your business more scalable, predictable and valuable, by building a set of 'Outstanding Operations' so that you have each and every process in the business documented.
- Help many more people whilst gaining more free time by cloning yourself; getting people to deliver your service as you would, time and again.

# Chapter 10: Delegate Your Way to Success!

*"If you really want to grow as an entrepreneur, you've got to learn to delegate."* Richard Branson

If you want to grasp your work life balance by the horns, and take back control of your life, there is one major key to your success. If you want the time to spend with the people who are important to you, have the opportunity to do the activities you enjoy most, and have the flexibility to keep yourself healthy, you've got to nail this section.

For a period of time, Caryl and two friends, Gilly and Liz, ran a cookery demonstration business called 'The Pink Figs.' They would go to people's houses, or invite people to theirs, in order to do a live demonstration of up to seven courses. The audience got to enjoy the produce of their labour, whilst learning how to cook and enjoying a glass or two of wine. It was very popular, but sadly they decided it was too much work during unsociable hours for the money it was generating. It was a shame, as they were all very talented and loved each other's company.

During that time, there was a constant steam of cookery programmes on our telly at home. Whether it was Jamie cooking Italian, wannabe chefs cooking for Gregg Wallace and John Torode, or Heston mastering the perfect lemon tart, the culinary shows never stopped. One day I remember watching Raymond Blanc. I am not sure what the show was called, but Raymond, the proud owner of two- Michelin stars, was preparing some delicate canapes for the show. He was stood at the table, in position, working his magic.

Stood behind Raymond was another chef. Are far as I could see, this sole responsibility of this man was to take things from the fridge and pass them to Raymond. Had the fridge been across the kitchen, I'd have probably never noticed this, but it wasn't. It was one stride away. Not even a big stride at that. Without difficulty, Raymond could have turned, taken one step, and retrieved the quail's eggs, or whatever was needed next, but he didn't.

He never left that table. His feet remained planted to the spot, and his hands never left the preparation table. He produced masterpiece after masterpiece in the 30-minute show using nothing but what Sir Ken Robinson would refer to as 'his element'. In his first TED Talk, 'How Schools Kill Creativity', the late Sir Ken Robinson talks about 'finding your element', also the title of his first book. Once you have found your element, you will never work a day in your life, you will just be following your passion.

Was he capable of retrieving things from the fridge? Of course! Could he have done a better job of retrieving from the fridge than his man in waiting? Again probably. Would it have been quicker for him to grab it than ask? Maybe, after all it was only a step away. So, why didn't he?

What Raymond has demonstrated is delegation. Most business owners are poor are delegation, as they are worried that they can do a better job, can do it more quickly than training someone else, and begrudge paying someone to do something they could have done themselves.

But Raymond evidently sees the benefit in delegation. Had he chosen to retrieve his items from the fridge, it would have taken him away from his element. He would have produced less in the 30 minutes allotted. He focused exclusively on his element, which was preparing amazing food, and that allowed him to deliver the maximum impact for his customers, and the audience. As a business owner you need to learn to do the same.

In the last chapter, we looked at how to create Outstanding Operations so that you can delegate more effectively. Once you have them in place, you can become better and better at delegating. When I ask members of my team to delegate a part of their role to someone else so that they can spend more time focusing on their element, they often find it difficult. They think it is something you are either good at or you are not. They think that I am a naturally good delegator. I am not; like anything though, it just took practice.

This reminds me of a joke with a message I tell Ffion and Bronwyn. I first read this in a Seth Godin book, although I can't honestly remember, or seem to be able to track down, which one.

This is the story: A worried looking 16-year-old girl is stood on a London street corner with a tattered violin case under her arm. A somewhat elderly gentleman in a long grey trench coat approaches her, and says in his frail voice, "Can I help you miss?"

"Oh, thank you" the girl stammers nervously, "could you possibly tell me how I get to the Royal Concert Hall please?"

"Yes Miss, I can" he replies, "the best way to get to the Royal Concert Hall is through practice practice, practice!"

I love that joke, and fortunately so do my girls. Whilst being mildly amusing, it has such a powerful message: A message that I have read more and more about in recent years. Whether you read Malcolm Gladwell's excellent 'Outliers', Anders Ericsson's brilliant 'Peak' or the unforgettable 'Bounce' by Matthew Syed, the evidence is clear. Firstly, name your book with one word... no, only joking, really the lesson is practice, practice, practice.

In 'Outliers', Gladwell talks about the need to reach 10,000 hours to become an expert; in 'Bounce' however, Syed says it is purposeful practice that really gains your progress. I love Gladwell's work, but I actually agree with Syed on this one: It isn't just about practice and allocating a certain amount of time. After all, I have spent huge amounts of time driving, even learning at the ripe old age of 7 whilst growing up on the farm, but that does not make me Lewis Hamilton. It isn't just about practice; it is about purposeful practice. In 'Peak', Ericsson takes this concept a step future: Even better than purposeful practice, it is actually about 'deliberate practice'. Purposeful practice becomes deliberate when it's guided and within a well-developed field.

So many people believe that the geniuses of the modern world were born as naturally gifted people. Whether it be David Beckham, Mozart, the William's sisters or Bill Gates, it is easy for us to believe that they were born that way. This simply isn't true. They worked hard to create their talent. Essentially, they put themselves in a position where they could get more purposeful practice than anyone else.

Let's take Mozart, for example. Despite popular misconception, even Mozart was trained, not just talented. His father was a very talented composer, and a very hard task master and, as a result, Mozart just happened to receive excellent training, starting before he was four years old. Also contrary to popular belief, Mozart likely only started composing 'proper' music in his teenage years. His earlier work was essentially reworkings of other music around at the time. Even that shows signs that it could have actually been the work of his father. By the time Mozart became a teenager he had had more deliberate practice than anyone else around at the time, because by then, he had put in a decade's worth of deliberate practice already.

In her magnificent book 'Mindset', Carol Dweck looks at the difference between a 'growth mindset' and a 'fixed mindset'. I am delighted that this book seems to be a topic of conversation in someone of the leading schools in the country, because for me it contains a very powerful message. Those people that have a 'fixed mindset' believe that you are either naturally good at something, or you aren't. This is a dangerous belief, as it causes you to accept what is, rather than to change it to what you want. A 'growth mindset' on the other hand, always believes you can get better and better; you just need the right practice at whatever it is you want to improve.

Caryl and Ffion are both talented artists. Not because they are born that way, but because over the years they have continued to do 'deliberate practice'. My artistic skills on the other hand are weak. I struggle to draw the curtains. However, I don't believe that I could not learn to draw. Coming to it later in life I may be slower to learn, but I could still massively improve. I could even become an amazing artist if I created the right opportunity for deliberate practice.

In 'Peak', Ericsson talks about a man deciding to take up golf at the age of 30. He didn't just want to be a golfer down the local club however, he wanted to be a tour professional by the age of 40. Is that possible? I have been playing golf since I was 13, so how can he pick up a club for the first-time aged 30 and reach professional status 10 years later? You guessed it, deliberate practice. He found a coach that could build him a programme that could create the perfect opportunity for him to progress at the right speed.

Amazingly, he didn't start hitting a golf ball with an iron or a wood for the first 3 months. The first three months was all about putting. Afterall, nearly half of your shots in golf are played with a putter. If he wanted to master golf, he needed to start with mastering putting. Then he started to hit the ball some distance with clubs. For each club however, he had key performance figures. Remember the importance of knowing your numbers! He knew what percentage he missed with his left or right hand, and with what club, so again he knew exactly what he needed to work on with his deliberate practice. Whilst 'Peak' was written before this chap reached the age of 40, he was on track to become a tour professional. Even if he didn't make it, he will definitely be the best golfer in his local club by then! Now that is a growth mindset if ever I saw one.

Going back to my original point, I was not a good delegator, but by reading books like 'The E-Myth Revisited' and going on programmes like The Strategic Coach® and Business Mastery, I got plenty deliberate practice. I learned how to delegate, and now I find it very easy. Caryl might even say I find it too easy! I would far rather pay someone to do our gardening than to do it myself. Not because I cannot do it, but because it isn't my element. Not only is a professional gardener going to do a better job than I am, they have the right tools for the job, and they enjoy it. Much better to pay someone who's element is working with their hands in the garden to do it, than to have me doing something that I have zero interest in.

Delegation is not just about getting people who are better than you to do a particular role. It is about giving you the opportunity to get deliberate practice in order to continue to perfect your element. TED talks, which I mentioned in Chapter 8, feature some of the worlds most respected minds imparting their 18 minutes of wisdom. They have been done by Richard Branson, Tony Robbins, Bill Gates, Bono, Jamie Oliver, Bill Clinton and Stephen Hawking, to name just a few. Strange then that the most watched TED talk of all time is by a Scouser with a passion for education.

The key to being successful in business is to find the things that you are a) really good at, and b) you really enjoy, and only do those things. Delegate everything else. I do this through regularly using 'Delegator Compound' exercise. You may not be able to do so immediately, but create a plan so that you can. However, to do that you need to know all the things you currently do, so let's start with that. Look back over the last week, month and year and list the jobs that you have been doing whilst at work. List everything, from checking your emails to changing the toilet rolls.

This isn't always easy looking backwards, so you may need to have this sat on your desk for the next week or more, so you don't miss anything.

Once done, take all of these jobs and put them into 1 of 4 categories:

1. Jobs you love and are great at
2. Jobs you love but aren't that good at
3. Jobs you dislike but you are great at
4. Jobs you don't like, and you aren't that good at

You should now have a list of jobs in each section. You will notice that box 1 contains all the jobs you are great at, and you enjoy. In that box you will probably be looking straight at what 'your element'. The stuff that gets you excited in the morning, and the stuff that is at the core of your business, and the likely reason you got into it in the first place. At the other end of the scale, the jobs in box 4 are the jobs you hate and that you really aren't very good at. Maybe you once enjoyed them, and maybe you used to think you were good at them, but now you don't.

Now we move onto the fun bit. Step 3. Identify ways to delegate all of the items in category 4, and as many in category 3 as possible.

When I first did this, I thought this was a one-off exercise. I went through the list in box 4, and overtime I delegated every one of those roles. Then I realised I needed to start to delegate the items listed in boxes 2 and 3 too. Some I had to retain, because of the regulatory nature of our business, but I got rid of most. When I came back to this exercise again a few of years later, I didn't think there was anything left I could delegate, but guess what, there was loads, because, what happens is that over time, you break jobs down into more granular parts.

For example, I initially had 'running the business' as one of my tasks. Overtime that has been broken down into many smaller parts, and that allows me to delegate more and more of that role. As a result, I now go through this exercise once a year. Each time I go into it thinking, 'I just cannot delegate any more of my roles out', and each year I identify significant amounts of each role that I can delegate. What this means is that over time I am refining down my element and asking other people to do all but those elements; people that in the most part are better at them than me.

I'd encourage you to do the same, and repeat on an annual basis. Do you think that when Raymond Blanc was originally recruiting at the start of launching Le Manoir aux Quatre Saisons, he thought he needed a 'fridge-assistant?'. Of course not! But over time he realised that even stepping away from his workstation reduced the amount of time he spent doing his element, and so that's when he recruited him.

As I've already said, not only does having a 'fridge assistant' allow you to spend more time doing what you do best to maximise its impact and allow you to perfect that even more by doing it more than anyone else, it is also the key to claiming back your work life balance. It is the one thing that allows your business to continue to grow, without it being at your own expense!

## Outsourced Efficiency
*"It always seems impossible until it's done."* Nelson Mandela

The wonderful thing about The Delegator Compound exercise, is that the more I do it, the more profitable we become. If I am left to do the bits I am best at, and others are allowed to do the bits that they are better at than me, it makes sense that we can all do more of those roles and make more money. However, I appreciate that when you first do this, you may not have immediately have sufficient team members to delegate all roles. Someone once said to me that you should employ the next person when you think you can fill 50% of their time, and you'll soon find things to fill the rest once they are onboard. That then gives you 50% of your time back, where you can fill more of your time with profitable activities, which capitalise on your element, to justify the cost.

That said, I appreciate you may have financial constraints that stop you just going out and hiring more people, or logistical constraints that means you cannot recruit the right people quickly. The wonderful thing today is that there is likely to be a technological solution that might fit the bill. Over the years we have outsourced some of our work to other companies in the UK, but also to people working in Argentina, the Philippines, and India, to name just a few. Clearly certain activities need to be done by people who are based in your home country, but many do not. For example, you can have a virtual assistant who takes care of most of your life, without even having an employment contract. You can also harness the power of AI to streamline and improve certain jobs and tasks.

Outsourcing is so good that I founded a business that does it for my former competitors. Accelerate Adviser Solutions specialises in providing paraplanning and administrative support to Financial Advisers all around the UK. The core aim of this business is to give advisers more time to spend on their clients, their business and themselves. If that's your business, and you'd like their help, please visit them at **www.accelerateteam.co.uk**

I have used a number of providers for outsourcing over the years. If you need someone that is specific to your industry, like paraplanning is to Financial Advisers, then you need to track down that specialist. If not, the best site I have found to source people is **www.upwork.com**. The sheer number of people and the information available about their work is incredible. We have employed people to do video editing, online research, data entry, calls, marketing campaigns, and many other tasks, and we have identified the best ways to achieve this. Here are my top tips to getting outsourcing to work for you:

1. Use the Upwork filters to screen for the right people.
2. Test their understanding with a simple question.
3. Give the top 3 candidates a task that relates to your project as a test.
4. Give your chosen candidate a probation period project.

It is amazing what you can get done, and the team you can build around you, without ever employing anyone. Don't let employing people stop you delegating!

## Outsourced Inbox

One on the biggest drains on business owners, and society for that matter, is our inbox. Many years ago, when I was launching The Rural Business Community, a rural serviced office in Rutland based on a farm in the village of Seaton in Rutland, I had to email the MD of BT Business.

Caryl and I had moved into the farmhouse at Seaton, and Efficient Portfolio had grown to a size where we needed more space. We had a redundant hay barn in the farmyard, a wonderful old stone building that was used as a dumping ground for old gates and the like, which was going to ruin. It would make a perfect home for Efficient Portfolio but would be too big for just us; after all we only had a team of 3. I decided to create The Rural Business Community, which was essentially designed to be our perfect office, but to also offer the same facilities and services as I had seen being offered in London. In rural Rutland, there wasn't anything like that at the time.

Seaton is a small village, with around 250 residents, and Rutland is the smallest and more rural country in England. Expecting fast broadband there in 2011 was probably foolhardy, but to make The Rural Business Community work, we had to have it. To make matters worse, the village was the furthest from the exchange, and the farm the furthest from the cabinet. It was treacherously slow, and not suitable to run a business on, let alone offer services to others.

I explored many different ways to get fast broadband in the year it took us to develop the barn into our new home. I looked at satellite broadband, broadband over electric powerlines and digging a trench around the entire village, amongst other things, as I was determined it wasn't going to beat me.

Through my conversations with BT and trying to get them to update to our exchange, I somehow ended up getting the email address of the MD of BT Business. I cannot quite remember how, but I sent him an email about the possibility of us upgrading our village to faster broadband. To my surprise, he replied, and not just once. We ended up having an email conversation until about 1 o'clock in the morning about Seaton's broadband. Now this was great for me, because at the time this was the biggest hurdle I had in getting The Rural Business Community off the ground, but was that time well spent for him? I couldn't help thinking that Seaton's broadband made no real difference to whether he did well in his role, and certainly whether BT did well as a business. I concluded that he needed as much help with his work life balance as anyone I knew. Didn't he have better things to do at 1 am than speak to me on email; and if not, why not?

If he was a one off, then there wouldn't be a story here. The problem is, he isn't. Most business owners, and now employees too, are a slave to their inbox. We all know we look at our phones too much, but looking at your business inbox in the evening is just wrong. In fact, I'll go further than that: Looking at your business inbox as the business owner, is always wrong.

In this day and age, there is so much spam and marketing nonsense that finds its way into our inbox, that we are bogged down by it. On the flip side of this, some people just ignore it and when they look at their phone they have 3587 emails still in their inbox, and then they wonder why they miss things! Others spend their life fighting a losing battle of whether they should reply to this email now or later.

I almost never look at my inbox. I haven't for over 12 years now. I know what you are thinking, boy, there must be a lot of emails in there by now! Clearly, I could not run a successful business if someone and something wasn't doing this on my behalf. Here are the secrets to my success.

Step 1: Unsubscribe to anything you don't look at almost every time you receive it. Yes, you might miss an offer for 10% off your next pair of jeans, but the time and stress you'll save in going through deleting 100 emails a day will more than compensate, I promise.

Step 2: Use 'Rules' to divert certain messages from certain people, into specific folders. I have a folder called 'Team' that automatically receives any emails from anyone in my team. I have another that is linked to our members, so that I don't miss their communications. Minimise the amount of time it takes to organise your emails by using technology, wherever possible.

Step 3: Set up multiple email addresses. For example, I have **news@efficientportfolio.co.uk**. Anything that sounds like a newsletter will be subscribed to this email address. That way, I can set up another 'Rule' to divert those emails automatically into a 'News' folder.

Step 4: Only your Personal Assistant or your Virtual Assistant get to look at your inbox. If you don't have a PA or a VA, reread the last section, and then find one on **www.upwork.com**. You'll be amazed at how little it will cost you.

Step 5: Create a 'Focus' folder, and a 'Buffer' folder, and draw out clear instructions as to what types of emails go into each. Also draw out clear instructions as to what can be delegated and to whom. This is a good example of an 'Outstanding Operation'.

Buffer emails are anything that isn't urgent, that if you don't read for 2 weeks, it won't hurt. Tell your PA/VA to check your emails 3 times a day and at each point, ask them to delegate to a team member, as per your instructions, or delete or file the rest in the relevant folder. Aim for no more than 3 focus email a day from your PA/VA.

Step 6: Check your Focus and Team emails 3 times a day. This allows you to focus on what's important for the rest of the day. At a set time, no more than once a week, review your news and buffer folders. Be ruthless at clearing stuff out quickly. Unsubscribe from anything that isn't important, as it will save you and your PA/VA time later. You may even want to adopt using a platform like 'Teams', the business equivalent of 'Whatsapp', to communicate with your team to prevent too many emails from this front.

Step 7: Sit back and watch the magic happen; you've just got a whole chunk of your life back. Your daily emails will drop from 100 to the 3 you see in 'Focus', plus any communications with your team.

For many people, this one thing can be a complete game changer, but for others it is just a starting point. There are many triggers that can lead to distraction, including your environment and technology, but many of these can be leveraged to your advantage if you use the right strategies.

Implementing these strategies requires commitment and discipline, but the payoff is immense. By creating an environment that promotes focus, understanding your distraction triggers, and using technology to support rather than hinder your work, you can significantly boost your productivity.

At The Trusted Team, we use a tool called 'The Productivity Focuser' to help you identify what distracts you and how you can overcome these barriers. If you'd like to learn more about this, why not book in for a free coaching call? Just email **hello@thetrusted.team** to select the best time.

## Delegation Success Strategies
*"Always make your future bigger than your past."* Dan Sullivan

Delegating aspects of your business can be a scary thing. Initially I found it very difficult, but overtime, I have got much better at it. It comes back to 'practice, practice, practice'. It is difficult to pass over a job that you know you can do, to someone who you aren't yet sure can do it quite as well. It is a psychological barrier that you need to get over, but there are some ways to make it easier.

Firstly, this is a tricky one, but you have to accept they are going to make some mistakes at some point. That said, so do you. No one is perfect, as it is easy to justify our own mistakes, because we can see the other factors involved. Even if they make a mistake more often than you, the importance of you giving up these tasks is so great, that this is a price worth paying.

Secondly, create amazing processes, or Outstanding Operations as I call them, that are full of checklists to ensure mistakes are minimal.

Thirdly, like Disney, create a decision-making process for the team. Across my businesses, we ask ourselves:

1. Is it Legal?

2. Is it compliant and ethical?

3. Does it keep the business viable to deliver what we do best?

4. Is it in the client's best interests?

5. Is it the team's best interests?

If your team follow this process, they should arrive at the right decision. Why not create one for your company?

In addition to identifying the aspects of your overall role that you can delegate, revisit this when you create your task list for the week ahead. More about this concept later on, but when you look down your to do list each day/week, firstly think about which of those roles you could delegate. If you can delegate them, ensure that you create an 'Outstanding Operation' for it, so that you never have to do it again!

Delegating as much of the roles you put in boxes 2,3 and 4 as possible will allow you to expand beyond your wildest dreams and will mean that you have far more free time than you've ever had before. Over time, you're 'box 1' roles will also probably change, and by repeating the delegation exercise time and again, you can constantly ensure that you are doing the best role for yourself and your business.

If you keep 'rinsing and repeating' this exercise over the years, it will gradually transform your business. If you want freedom, master delegation!

Earlier in this chapter I mentioned The Delegate Compound tool. If you'd like a guided talk through this exercise, and complete your own, the best place to see this in action is at my free 3 Steps to Entrepreneurial Happiness virtual workshop. To register, please visit **www.thetrusted.team/virtual-workshops**

## Chapter Summary

- If you truly want to get more of your time back, you need to identify better ways to delegate. As a business owner, you need to learn to become an expert delegator.
- Easily upscale your business and achieve more without taking on another employed person by using outsourced solutions.
- Give yourself more freedom by delegating your inbox.

# Chapter 11: Energy Abound

*"Energy is the key to creativity. Energy is the key to life."*
William Shatner

People often ask me, "where do I get my energy from?" In addition to running a number of businesses, taking 12 weeks of holiday a year with the family, and doing the school run at least a couple of times a week, I also take part in multiple Ironman and endurance events, which often involve a 2.4-mile swim, 112-mile bike and then a 26.2-mile run.

Because a significant part of my role is finding new clients, building new relationships, and learning new skills to drive the business forward, I do end up attending a number of breakfast and evening seminars, and international conferences. This makes family time and training difficult, but both are important enough to make sure they happen.

A typical week for me is to be up at 5.30 every day. I swim roughly 3km Monday, Wednesday, and Friday morning. I cycle twice a week for around 20 miles, and I ride of about 60-100 miles once per week. I also run 3 times per week, covering 7 miles on 2 of the days, plus I also complete a longer run on the third. All that takes a lot of time.

In addition, at work I need to be full of energy, because when you are leading a team, creating coaching content, or building businesses, which are my 3 main roles in the, I need to have energy. That's because, in every instance, they feed off my energy. If I am lacklustre, the results will also reflect that.

Don't get me wrong, if like yesterday, where I was presenting at breakfast meeting at 7am, running 5 miles at lunchtime, and then presenting again at a speaker event until 8pm, I am usually tired by bedtime. That said, this morning, I was in the pool swimming 3km again, because I have the energy to do so.

It wasn't however always like this. Not so many years ago I was into playing squash. It was the one thing that kept my excess weight getting even worse. Typically, I played in the evening, but it was tricky organising some of the league games. Inevitably, occasionally I would suggest that we played before work, if it was the only way we could get the game in before the end of the month. The funny thing was that my squash, normally a reasonable level, was appalling at this time of the morning. I remember losing matches and missing shots that would have been easy wins in the evening.

During these early morning games, which were being played at 7.30am, my coordination was off, I tired more easily, and my strategic play was dreadful. Interestingly, for some of my opponents, they were equally as bad. If you want to run a healthy business, you need to run a healthy body, and also have a healthy team around you. If you want to have an energised business, you need to be an energised person, and have an energised team. If you want to have a happy team, you need to be a happy leader.

The question you are probably asking though is, what changed? Why just a few years ago, when I was obviously younger than I am now, did I have less energy than I have today? As I told you in my story, it all started at 'Unleash the Power Within'- the Tony Robbins event that involved fire walking and The Dicken's process. When asked to look at my life 20 years from now, if it had continued as it was at that moment, and I had continued making the same decisions as I was at that time, I might be telling a very different story now.

I envisioned a one-bedroom flat, with me sitting slumped in a chair, with my gut hanging over the side, surrounded by pizza boxes- it was a sight of pure pain. Caryl and the girls had left me, all of businesses had long since folded, and all the things that I loved had left my life. That is pretty good leverage to make some significant changes. And it was leverage that was the key. I needed a big enough reason to change.

As Tony says, if you asked a smoker to give up smoking tomorrow, they'd tell you it was difficult, and maybe impossible for them to achieve. If you then put a gun to their head and asked them the same question, suddenly it becomes a lot easier. It is all about the leverage! If it is important enough, you will do it, the question is how do you make it important, how do you give yourself the leverage?"

That is exactly what Tony did for me. Firstly, he facilitated me identifying the error of my current ways, through what he calls 'limiting beliefs'. He then gave me that future vision, which was my leverage to make a significant change. If you want to change, you need to do the same.

In order that you can create the leverage to ensure you do take your health seriously and achieve the results you know you want and need, I have put together an exercise for you to work through. This can be found in The Entrepreneurial

Happiness Workbook, that you can download for free from **www.thetrusted.team/books/entrepreneurial-happiness**.

Don't get me wrong, going through this exercise on a form in a book is in no way supposed to replace the power of doing this at an event like Unleash the Power Within (UPW). However, it is the best I can do from here. If you want to make some significant changes to your personal life, I cannot encourage you enough to attend UPW. It certainly changed my life.

As a combination of UPW and other courses I subsequently attended, I realised I had leant a number of important strategies. In summary I suppose, they were a way to look after my body better, the way to make the right decisions stick, and a way to be happier. When I first created this, I called it 'The Healthy Life 2.0 System', and it's made up of 3 sections: Body, mind and relationships. Each of these areas has the ability to make a massive difference in your business and personal life. Clearly you could write a whole book on each of these subjects, and many people have, but here is a whistle-stop tour for those short on time.

## The Age Reversal Revolution

As the adage goes, if you don't make time for health, you'll have to make time for illness! Ever since aging was classified as a disease, research into halting and even reversing it has progressed rapidly. While some of these scientific breakthroughs may not be mainstream yet, there are concrete steps you can take today to slow down and potentially reverse aging, whilst significantly improving your health today.

As a business owner, your most precious asset is your health. If you have your health, you have a thousand dreams for your company. But if you lose your health, you only have one dream left - to regain it. There's no point in building a successful enterprise if you don't have your vitality to enjoy the fruits of your labour. Make time for your wellness today, or you'll be forced to make time for illness down the road.

You truly do have two entrepreneurial lives - the second begins when you realise you only get one shot at robust health. That wake-up call often comes in our 40s when we start thinking about self-care before it's too late. The good news is that by extending your 'healthspan'- the years you remain full of vitality and disease-free - you can dramatically extend your productive lifespan too.

The key is prevention over cure. The future of health is stopping illnesses like cancer, Alzheimer's, heart disease, and diabetes before they take root by treating their upstream cause - aging itself. A wellspring of emerging technologies will make that possible in our lifetimes if we embrace them.

From regenerative stem cell treatments to 3D printed organs, from wearable diagnoses to genetic therapies, our ability to renew and fortify our bodies is accelerating rapidly. We're uncovering the molecular mechanisms underlying aging and how to buffer them through precision lifestyle strategies. The coming era of personalised medicine, tailored to your unique biochemistry and health data, will be a game-changer.

Imagine having an AI nutritionist that scans your meal and forecasts its impacts on your biomarkers. Or smart home sensors that automatically course-correct your environment for restorative sleep. Having your personal 'data cloud' continuously analysed will enable catching imbalances early and nudging you toward better choices.

While genetics may load the gun, your daily habits are pulling the trigger when it comes to outrunning age-related diseases. You can't control inherited risks, but you can mitigate them through purposeful living.

Of all longevity promoters, physical exercise is the closest thing to a fountain of youth we have. Aerobic fitness measured by VO2 max is one of the best predictors of extended healthspan. The good news is you don't need to be an athlete - just doing 90 minutes of vigorous cardio a week can cut your mortality risk by 14%. Simple strength training also becomes increasingly vital as we age for maintaining muscle mass and avoiding frailty.

Consistent moderate exercise, smart nutrition, stress management, and strategic supplementation can pay huge dividends over time in extending your productive years. Even small upgrades to your standard of living can yield an enormous 'longevity dividend.'

Humanity is approaching 'longevity escape velocity' - the point where therapies extend your remaining lifespan faster than you age biologically. This could be the first generation to break aging itself. In this dawning age of longevity, health is the purest wealth. The real risk is succumbing to preventable illness or decline before reaching that horizon.

We're in the midst of a vitality revolution - one that discerning entrepreneurs can't afford to ignore.

At The Trusted Team we use a tool called 'The Age Reversal Revolution'. The Age Reversal Revolution provides actionable strategies to bolster your health, decelerate aging, and boost your performance. Book your free coaching call to find out more by emailing **hello@thetrusted.team**

## A Happy Perspective

*"Many of us die at 30 but are buried at 80."* Robin Sharma

As a business owner, there is always bad news. There is bad news in the press, there is that client who turns their back on you, or the prospect that refuses to take your advice. If you don't have thick skin, these can all get you down. If you read too much bad news, it can paralyse you into not taking action, and this stops you improving as a business. A worried and stressed business owner or partner does not make a good leader, as that fear translates across your team.

One thing that can easily get the most resilient entrepreneur down is bad news, so let's talk about kicking the constant news habit of today's society. After all, NEWS does stand for 'Negative Events World Service'! In today's world of 24/7 news, it is easy to get caught up in watching the news three times a day, reading the paper and catching up online. Many would say that this is allowing you to be informed and up to date with today's important stories, and I can appreciate that argument, but does it make you happy? Only a small fraction of all news that you consume is good news. Is that because good things don't happen? Of course not, good things happen all the time, but bad news makes good news, as they say.

I would argue that consuming this level of news, particularly when you are unlikely to do anything about it, only serves the purpose of draining your happiness. Let's take Covid as a poignant example. The impact of the pandemic devastated communities and countries, led to huge losses of life, and caused catastrophic economic damage.

Medical professionals, be it doctors, nurses or research scientists were, and still are, heroic, and we shouldn't ignore news of their work, but if you consumed news all day long, especially during 2020-2023, what was your brain absorbing? You would have heard about Covid first thing, then again at lunch, and then again just before you go to bed, when you read the paper or online articles, and perhaps even while you are driving.

Did the Covid situation change that much between each of those meals or events? Maybe during the early days of lockdowns it did, but not much. Could you have got all of the same information by reading one article, or watching one piece of news a day, or even one per week? You would have probably got a more rounded understanding, because instead of rehashing the news each time to make it slightly different, you would have instead got the bigger picture all in one go.

Clearly, when you are working, you need to keep up with what is relevant to your field. If you are a banker, you need to read the *Financial Times* as part of your job. I used to need to know financial services news so that I could give the best advice to my clients. But I didn't need to hear doom and gloom all day, every day.

Since I started to take this approach about three years ago, I know nearly as much as I did beforehand (and on the topics important to me, I know even more), but I am also far happier. As Matt Ridley suggests in *The Rational Optimist*, 'Most of the bad news will never happen anyway. How many times has bird flu or swine flu been about to kill thousands, but it never happens? It's even worse in the world of finance. As the saying goes, Economists have predicted 12 of the last 3 recessions!' Matt Ridley says you can be a pessimist, and possibly be right but miserable, or you can be an optimist and possibly be right but be happy. I know which I prefer.

In '*The Rational Optimist*', Ridley also discusses the gap between reality and our perceptions. When surveyed, most people felt that murder rates were on the rise, due to the increased publicity of each death. But when you look at the reality of the situation (see Ridley's chart), you realise that compared to 700 years ago, murders are almost non-existent today. It's all about perception!

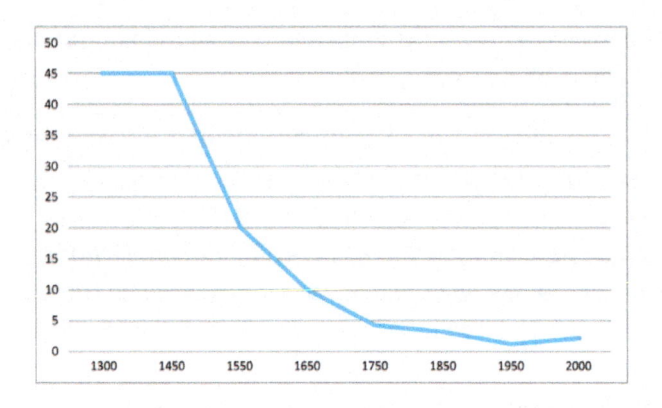

Initially when taking the approach of not consuming as much news, you think you might miss something important. You won't. That guilt is soon replaced with a feeling of contentment. How many people go to sleep where the last thing they have watched is about a war-torn part of the world on the 10 o'clock news, and then the first thing they watch over their bowl of cereal is the very same topic? Most of the time, nothing has changed!

In today's world, it is also very easy to set up a stream of specific news that is important to you. For example, I set up a Threads feed that provides me with a constant stream of business news. I can look anytime I want, but I am not bombarded with it when I don't, like on my 'Free Days' (more on that in a bit). You can look at specific publications, whether that be online or through traditional media. That way you can consume news as and when you want to, without constantly infecting your brain with global misery.

If you want to ensure you don't get left behind, I can highly recommend the magazine called *The Week*. In a weekly magazine, you can read all of the news stories from the previous 7 days, from a diverse spread of publications. All the news you need in one hit, and then you are free to enjoy the rest of your life without worry! There are of course easy ways to do the same online, using apps like *Flipboard*, where you can effectively build your own personal newspaper for free. I encourage you to give it a try. Opt out of the mainstream and conventional news and replace the guilt with happiness!

## The Giver of Gratitude

*"Happiness Equals Reality Minus Expectations."* Tom Magliozzi

It is impossible to feel anger when you are feeling grateful. In her excellent book Thrive, Arianna Huffington talks about documenting what she is grateful for each day. By doing this, she has found herself a lot happier.

Caryl, my wife, is part of a gratitude club on Facebook. Full of likeminded people that she met on a mindfulness course, each day she, and others, share what they are grateful for. By doing this, you are again focusing on the positives in your life, even during times of extreme negatives. A lot these should be about the simple things in life, for example, the fact that the sun is shining, that you live in a safe country or that you have a wonderful pet dog!

In a business sense, by focusing on the things in life you are grateful each day, you can take a step closer to entrepreneurial happiness. Whether you do this as part of writing a journal each morning, a Facebook group of likeminded people, using an App like 'Grateful' or in your head while you are exercising or meditating, make sure you do. It is a wonderful gift to the soul.

In my Better Future Framework, I get people to do exercises called 'The Best Things' and 'The Gratitude Gateway' to help them become happier and more positive. You can find out more about this at **www.thetrusted.team/bff**. I also teach these exercises in more depth at The Trusted Team Workshops and at the free Limitless Life Workshop. If you'd like to know more about the latter, please visit **www.thetrusted.team/the-limitless-life-workshop**

## The 6 Human Needs

*"If the only tool you have is a hammer, you tend to see every problem as a nail."* Abraham Maslow

Tony Robbins is world renowned for helping people get a better perspective on life. In his book 'Unshakeable' he talks about Robin Williams. Do you love the work of Robin Williams? I certainly do. People don't tend to just like him, they love him. He was infectious in his comedy, in a way that transcends generations. Whether it is the hilarious Mrs Doubtfire, the belly laughing Patch Adams or the screaming of 'Gooooooooodddddd Mooooooooooorrrniiingggg Viiiieeetttnaaammm', you just can't help but love what he did!

Robin Williams set out to have his own TV show, and he achieved that. He wanted to make the show no.1 in the US, and he achieved that too. He strived to create a wonderful family, and he achieved that. He set his heart on becoming a movie star, and he did that. He then dreamt of becoming an Academy Award winner for a serious film, when his forte was comedy, and he did that. He achieved everything he set himself, and then he hung himself after being misdiagnosed with Parkinson's and falling into a state of depression.

Robin Williams, like so many people had mastered the 'Science of Achievement' as Tony puts it, but he never mastered the 'Science of Fulfilment'. When you are on a plane, and you get the safety briefing at the start, so they tell you to put the oxygen mask on your child first? No, they don't, they tell you to put it on yourself first. You have to help yourself first. You have to be happy in yourself before you can help others become happy; as a business owner, one of your roles is to make your team and clients happy.

Sadly, Robin Williams never mastered the 'Art of Fulfilment'. How can such a master of making other people happy never master the art of making himself happy? It is so sad. One of the principles we spent time focusing on at Unleash the Power Within, is the '6 Human Needs'. Based on 'Maslow's Human Needs', Tony enhanced and improved this to create his own version. Let's look at them through a business owner's eyes.

### 1. Certainty

In order to be happy, we need 'Certainty' in our life. We need to know our business is safe for the future, and that we have sufficient income to pay our bills. If we don't have 'Certainty' in our business and personal life, we will be distinctly unhappy, as it will cause huge levels of stress.

### 2. Uncertainty / Variety

We also need life to be different, or uncertain. If you do the same thing in your business day in day out, you will become bored. You need to create variety if your life, otherwise you will lose your motivation to do what you do.

### 3. Significance

We all need to feel significance; the question is just how much. A business owner with a team around them often feels significant, as they have a team of people trying to help him achieve their goals. That said, if you don't have a team, or your team are not helping you as much as they should, a lack of significance will start to get you down. This is no more obvious than when business owners get together socially, and they are all trying to show that they are the most significant!

### 4. Connection / Love

In life we all need 'Connection' to others. In your personal life, hopefully you get as far as 'Love' but in business you need to be spending your time with people you like. Whether that be your clients or your team, if you are not spending your time around people you want to be with, you will be an unhappy entrepreneur.

Those four 'Human Needs' are your core needs. Everyone needs these addressed if they want to be happy; however, to be truly happy, you also need to satisfy the final two 'Human Needs'.

### 5. Growth

If you aren't growing, you are dying. For a business owner, if you are not getting better, you are falling behind. If your business isn't continually innovating, you are losing ground on the competition. If you are not improving as a person, you too are losing ground.

### 6. Contribution

Finally, to be truly happy you need to feel that you are making a contribution. Whether that is improving the lives of your clients, your team or the charitable work that comes out of your company, is up to you.

Each person has differing demands in each area. You will also have one or two areas that are most important to you, that is unless one is not being satisfied at all. For example, perhaps 'Significance' is your most important 'Human Need', however if suddenly you lose your certainty because of a recession, that will temporarily jump to the top of the pile until you get enough 'Certainty' for you to feel comfortable again.

To help you identify how well you are meeting each need and what you can do to improve each area, I have put together an exercise for you to work through. This can be found in The Entrepreneurial Happiness Workbook, that you can download for free from **www.thetrusted.team/books/entrepreneurial-happiness**.

This exercise is founded on my 'Human Needs Interrogator'. To apply these concepts effectively, you need to start by conducting a 'Human Needs Interrogation' for yourself and your team and assess how well each need is currently being met on a scale from 1 to 10. This will identify actions that could enhance the fulfilment of each need.

If you want to be truly happy, then you need to ensure that all of your 6 'Human Needs' are met, not just to their minimum level, but to your desired level. By looking at this each year, I find it allows me to see where my life is not quite delivering everything I want and need. I find it is a really good exercise to then allow me to highlight what I can change to make it even better. It is also a really good exercise to go through with your loved ones, as it helps you see how you could help them change their life to make them even happier.

## Chapter Summary

- In order to be the best business leader, you need to live a life that generates more energy, and that comes with taking your health seriously.
- If you want to have a healthy business, you need to have a healthy business owner and healthy team.
- The best way to achieve this is to create massive leverage; a hugely compelling reason why you must become the healthiest you can be.
- Take a step towards a healthier future by following The B.E.T.T.E.R. Body system.
- To truly embrace Entrepreneurial Happiness, you need to be content and happy in yourself. You can achieve this by focusing on 'The Best Things' and the things you are grateful for.
- Better understand what makes you happy by understanding 'The 6 Human Needs'.

# Chapter 12: A Life Less Ordinary

*"Not dead, can't quit."* Richard Machowicz

Until I thought of this chapter's title, I had totally forgotten about a fantastic film featuring Euan McGregor and Cameron Diaz of the same name. I will make a point of watching that again now, as I haven't revisited it since it was first released, when I was age 20. I loved that film, and having now Googled it, found out that it was a Danny Boyle film. Another brilliant film to add to his long list of hits. Whilst I thought this was a brilliant film over 20 years ago, I wonder if I will enjoy it as much when I get around to re-watching it. Have you ever found that time distorts our memories?

Time actually distorts reality. Often, what seemed brilliant years ago doesn't appear so today. Also, what seemed huge when you were younger, seems so small now. If you want to master entrepreneurial happiness, you need to master your time. There have been many great business books written on time management, which all seem to recount some good principles, but you need to read a lot on the topic to really grasp the concept as a whole.

They say that if you want something done, you should ask a busy person. This is so true. Those achievers seem to get so much more done than anyone else, and yet, as far as I am aware, we all only have 24 hours in the day to work with. How do they do it? People often ask me, where do I find the time for it all? Afterall, I take 12 weeks holiday a year with my family, I run 5 companies, I've written 4 books in the last 6 years, I've got my handicap down to 12 and I continually training for the next Ironman. It's all about time management and delegation. Delegation I have covered already, so let's look a little more deeply at time.

## Ripped Growth Energiser!
*"World class begins where your comfort zone ends."* Robin Sharma

I believe that to lead a truly happy life, you need to have 6 roles that touch upon your human needs, which I call 'The 6 Spheres of Success'. These are:

- Relationships
- On Business (Entrepreneur)
- Wealth
- Entrepreneur
- Health
- In Business (Your purpose)

What are my roles in life? What are my 6 Spheres of Success?

Firstly, and most importantly I am a husband and a dad. I need to keep myself in great shape, so that's another. In my business life I am primarily a business owner. I am then a coach and speaker, and then also a marketeer. That is 3 personal roles, and 3 business roles. I have clearly defined what each is, and even better, they each have a name. Want to know what they are? I admit they are somewhat cringeworthy, but when I see them, I know exactly what they sum up. Here goes me bearing my soul!

- Relationships: Super Dad & Hubbie
- On Business (Entrepreneur): The Entrepreneurial Spoke
- Wealth: Marketing Money Magnet *(slight cringe)*
- Happiness: Ultimate Life Designer
- Health: The Ironman
- In Business (Your purpose): The Performance Coach

These have been the names of my roles for roughly the last 10 years. When I build my goals, I build them for each of these roles. Every quarter, month and even week I set out goals that are going to deliver my 1 year and 3-year goals for each of these roles.

The reason this is so important, is for each of my small weekly goals I know that they are doing two things: Firstly, I know that they are a step towards my bigger goals, but secondly, they are a part of me living that role and why they are important.

For example, I hate checking another person's work. It is my least favourite activity at work, but sometimes that is what I have to do. That said, if it is part of me delivering amazing coaching to a client, and I know it is part of me being 'The Builder of Dreams' I am more excited to get it done. I cannot push it to the back burner, because that would be me failing in that role. It is my leverage, for every element of what I do.

To help you build better and more compelling goals I strongly recommend that you watch my Limitless Life

Workshop. It's virtual, so you can watch it from anywhere and it's completely free of charge. You can register here: **www.thetrusted.team/the-limitless-life-workshop**

## NE Time

*"My favourite things in life don't cost any money. It's really clear that the most precious resource we all have is time."*
Steve Jobs

When listing my business roles, you'll notice that I said that when it came to my business life, I said I was a business owner first and a coach second. I absolutely believe this has to be the case. If I want to be a coach first, I need to be employed, or pay for an MD to run my businesses. This is a mistake that many small business owners make. If you run your own business, you have to be a business owner first, and then your professional career is your second role. That means you need to read more on running a business than you do on being a professional.

If you get this bit wrong, you will likely fail, or at minimum, have a massively stressful business existence. If you only want to be your professional role, then you need someone else to be taking care of the running the business bit, because it is massively important. What good are your professional skills if your business fails?

If I take you back to Joe at Table R Us in the prologue, he was being a carpenter, not a business owner. His business coach taught him how to be a business owner, and he reengineered that business so that it ran far more professionally. That allowed him to carry on being the carpenter he wanted to be.

I am sure you are a great accountant, land agent, solicitor, whatever you are, but are you a great business owner? If you aren't, given it is your most important business role, what can you do about it. What books can you read to improve the way you see and run your business. Throughout this book I have given you many book recommendations, but later in this book I give you my top business books to read, so that would be a great start.

What courses could you book yourself on to learn more about your business? I'm obviously biased and would recommend joining my Trusted Team! It's not for everyone, as you really do need to play full out and commit yourself to implementing what I teach, but I know how much value it can add. If you don't believe me, why not check out what some our members have to say at **www.thetrusted.team/testimonials**.

Whatever it is that works for you, make sure you are spending a minimum of 1 day a quarter working on the business, rather than in it.

One flicker of resistance that you may now be feeling is, when do I have the time to do all this? Given that this is a chapter on time, I am glad you asked.

When it comes to reading, as I told you at the start, I have read over 250 business and personal development books and counting in the last few years, but where do I find the time? If I told you that as a dyslexic person, I am a hopelessly slow reader too, this would compound the problem, except it doesn't, because I read these books in NE Time. NE stands for 'No Extra' time.

'NE Time' is time that you were spending doing something else but where you can add in an extra activity, to buy yourself double the amount of time. The simplest example I can give you of this is how I read these books, or more accurately listened to these books. When I discovered audiobooks, it was a revelation, because suddenly I could consume books at the speed that everyone else does; but not only that, I could do so when I was doing other things. When I am in the car, on the bike or even running, I listen to books.

I used to just listen to 1 book at a time, but I've realised that different books work for me during different activities. For running, I need personal development or fitness. For driving and cycling I like business and marketing books, and for holidays I like biographies, with the odd drop of fiction thrown in.

I have also discovered another way to use audiobooks to enhance my NE Time: I now listen to different books at different speeds, for two reasons. Firstly, for some books, like business books, I need a little more thinking time, so I'll listen to them a 1.5x speed. I know that will sound fast to you initially, but the brain soon adapts to that.

Occasionally for a certain book I'll need to go back down to 1x speed, but it's rare now. When I am on a biography, where I don't need so much thinking time and the attention to detail, I'll up it to 2x speed. At this speed I am reading twice as many books as I used to be. Even at 1.5x I am reading four books in the time it previously read three. The second reason I listen to books at different speeds is that I have found that some books work better at different speeds. The best example of this that I can give you is Daniel

Kahneman's award winning book 'Thinking Fast and Slow'. Ironic name given what I am about to tell you.

I had heard a few people say how brilliant this book was, so I downloaded, and set about listening. I got about a chapter into what is a very long book: some 20+ hours no less, and lost interest. Then I read an article a year or so later listing the top business books of all time, and no. 3 was 'Thinking Fast and Slow'. I must revisit this I thought. Again, I got a chapter in, and I was losing interest. My mind would drift off elsewhere, and before I knew it, I had gone 5 minutes without listening to a word that had been said. It just wasn't working for me. It was at this time I had heard some say about changing your listening speeds, so I decided to have a play around with the speed on this book. Bizarrely, as soon as I set the speed to 1.5x, it became much more compelling. Suddenly, I was enjoying it and whilst it is still a long book, I listened to it avidly thereafter.

NE Time doesn't just apply to listening to books though. It can be applied to exercise too. So, how can you multitask your day? Caryl says that I cannot multitask, and in many ways she is right, but when it comes to listening to audiobooks, she is definitely wrong. I can absorb books while doing other things. Likewise, if I need to watch a webinar, I'll be thinking 'can I do this whilst sat on the exercise bike or treadmill?' Even when you are walking around between meetings, there is always NE Time. For example, walking down the escalators in the underground or taking the stairs in the office rather than the lift, not only do you possibly get to your destination faster, you've just squeezed some more exercise into your busy day, without giving it any time! Result. If one of the girls has a birthday party they need taking to, I will go for a run or a cycle while I wait. Don't just hang around reading the newspaper or looking at your phone, see that as an opportunity to fit in something important.

We waste a lot more time than we realise, and NE Time forces you to re-evaluate that. What can you do during your day in NE Time? If you think hard, I bet you can cram in a whole load more activities without it costing you any more.

## The Time System

I mentioned The Strategic Coach® Programme, which is something I found extremely beneficial for the 7 years I attended. As a result of attending my quarterly Strategic Coach® workshops, I learned to split my time up into three types of days—Free, Focus and Buffer Days®.

On my 'Focus' days, I only do the things that make us profitable. I only do these activities, nothing else, because it is better for me, my team and my clients that I work with this structure. In the early days this was difficult, but I would be allowed to do 80% 'Focus' activities, and 20% 'Buffer'.

At the time, my Focus activities were:

1. Seeing and speaking to clients.
2. Working on improving our business.
3. Working with and organising my team.


As the business has evolved, these too have evolved and are now:

1. Seeing our top clients.
2. Managing our business.

3. Marketing our business.
4. Thinking!

On my Focus Days, I am only allowed to do these activities, because this ensures that I maximise my time at work into only doing the parts of the job that I am best at.

Don't get me wrong, I need to do other tasks during a week, so these are reserved for my 'Buffer' days. On a Buffer day, I do anything else that is required, and if any 'Focus' activity happens too, then all the better. But it is these 'Buffer' days that allow me to be organised and effective on my 'Focus' days. Over time however, I have delegated more and more of the Buffer activities, which means I can now keep that to around ½ day per week.

Finally, I have my 'Free' days, where from midnight through to midnight I do not look at, engage in or think about work. This includes not checking emails! It does the mind good to have a break from a particular subject, and I am much better on my 'Focus' days as a result of these rules.

You too can apply this principle to your life by first determining what activities fall into the 'Focus' category for you. For example, it maybe that creating accounts is one of your key roles, because not only are you really good at it, you also enjoy it. If it is, that should be one of your Focus activities. Remember though, these activities should be the things that you are best at, enjoy, and that make the company money. If you go back to The Job List Delegator Exercise, these should ideally be the things in box 1.

The next, step is to build 'The Happy Week'. For me Mondays are about being in the office with my team, ensuring they are set for the week. This is a Focus Day for me as I am managing the business. It is also dedicated to organising myself, so that I can delegate things to my team and implement important priorities for the week. These have become my 'Team Focus' days.

Tuesdays are about seeing and speaking to clients and are my, wait for it, 'Client Focus' days. Wednesdays are my days for strategic planning and course creation, so are my 'Business Planning' Focus days. Thursdays are then left as my 'Marketing Focus' or 'Content Creation' days.

My 'Buffer' day is a Friday when I do anything else that needs doing. I expect to have this sufficiently well organised by the team so that it is all done by lunchtime, as Friday afternoon is my time for either cycling or golf.

Saturday and Sunday are my 'Free' days, where the family get my undivided attention. I am lucky enough to be able to say that I could count on one hand the number of weekends I have worked in recent years, other than when I attend a course or conference that happens to fall on those days, which is also rare now too.

By building 'The Happy Week', I have built certainty into my week as a matter of course. I know and my team knows where I am likely to be on any one day. They know when to book certain meetings, and I know that I have the certainty of a routine. Clients also know where I am likely to be and when, which gives them certainty too. It also means that I still get variety, as my 'Free' days are exactly that. They aren't invaded by work and can be spent with Caryl and our two beautiful girls, Ffion and Bronwyn.

I would encourage you to think about how you can use these strategies to build 'The Happy Week'. Don't get me wrong, this didn't happen overnight, it took time. It has continued to evolve, but if you don't start, you'll never get to this point. That's why you need to make a start now, and then revisit this again each year, to make sure you are sticking to it.

This allows you to be far more consistent, and that allows you to plan even further. You will remember that from the last chapter that I need to fit in 2 runs, 2 swims and 1 long or 2 shorter bike sessions. With a consistent work week, I could do this much more easily. I swim Monday, Wednesday, and Friday mornings, when Caryl is able to do the school run. I run Tuesday and Thursday mornings, so I can do the school run on those days. My business planning day is usually a long one, so that is my first rest day. I then cycle either alone on Friday afternoon or with friends on Saturday morning, depending on the weekend's plans. I said in the last chapter that simple rules are the key. If you can bring simplicity to your week, you will achieve so much more.

By building 'The Happy Week' for work, play and health, you will achieve so much more than most people. Research shows that generally we perform better in the morning than the afternoon, but that is different for everyone, so also think about which activities are best done when during the day. I will try and have client meetings, when I need to be on my A-Game in the morning, as I know I function better then than in the afternoon. In my coaching workshops, I get people to do an exercise called 'The Happy Week Worksheet' to help them design their perfect week, bother from a work personal and health perspective. If you'd like to learn more about this, please book in for a free call with me by emailing **hello@thetrusted.team**

Brian Tracy says that 'every hour spent in preparation saves ten hours in implementation'. Not only does planning save you time, but it is also more inherently rewarding, as you achieve increased productivity and ultimately have more time for yourself, and that leads me onto the next section nicely.

## Failing to Plan = Planning to Fail

After I'd been cycling for a just a few months, I joined up with some friends who were cycling from Rutland to London to raise money for charity. This was the first time I had cycled with anyone else, as until that point it all been alone. A couple of the group were experienced cyclists, so they were somewhat bemused with me when I rocked up on my mountain bike!

During the 30 or so miles I rode with them, a female cyclist decided she was too warm, and she needed to take off her jacket. Calm as you like, her hands left the handlebars and she continued cycling down the road. She then proceeded to remove said jacket, and tuck it into her back pocket, all without so much as a wobble. This was my first experience of cycling envy. That was cool, and I wanted to be able to do the same.

As a child growing up on the farm, I spent a fair amount of time on my bike, but I'd never mastered riding with no hands then, so what makes me think I should be able to now? Well, now I was armed with the knowledge of a 'growth mindset', as Carol Dweck describes it, so I knew I could master it. I also knew that if I wanted to achieve something, I needed to focus intently on the end goal, not the obstacles in the way.

Historically, when I tried to master riding a bike with no hands as a child, I had looked down at the road and the bike. These are the obstacles, not where I actually want to go. With this knowledge, I realised I needed a different approach. I needed to focus on where I wanted to go. I also realised that with 'practice, practice, practice', I could achieve anything I wanted to.

As a result, I repeatedly tried cycling with no hands when out on my own, every time focusing on the horizon ahead of me. Focusing on the prize or the goal as it were; and guess what happened. I mastered it, and I mastered it quickly. By aiming at the goal ahead of me with laser like focus, I was able to hit it. If you want to achieve what is important to you, you too need to have laser like focus on those goals. It's all very easy to write goals out and then forget about them. That doesn't ensure you hit them though. Constantly reminding yourself of what those goals are is more difficult, but this is what is needed if you want to achieve them.

What you can achieve distorts overtime. We overestimate what we can achieve in a short period of time, but we massively underestimate what we can achieve in a longer period of time. When I look back on the goals I was writing 10 years ago, they seem a lifetime ago. What I wanted to achieve in 10 years has easily been surpassed, but each quarter the goals I set seemed like a stretch, and I didn't always achieve them.

Writing down our goals is a vital strategy to success. Do you remember that in Chapter 4 I told you about the Harvard Graduates? This story illustrates what a massive difference goals make to what we achieve, and they also allow us to clarify our goals. It is extremely satisfying to set a goal and then to achieve it. You don't always hit the goal either, but as they say, if you shoot for the stars, you might hit the moon!

That is why your cornerstone for a more successful future is great goal setting and management. I've heard it said that 'losers have goals, winners have systems', and this is so right. Whilst just writing down the goal is better than nothing, clearly you need a better strategy if you really want to achieve them. That is where 'The Life Planner' comes in. This is a document that I have built up over the years to help me on a day-to-day basis to ensure I hit my bigger goals.

You see, if you want to create an amazing future, you need to have some big lifetime goals, but you also need to have shorter term goals that will get you there. 90 days, or one quarter of the year is a great timeframe to build your goals around, as you can keep momentum and focus relatively easy over this duration; however, after 90 days you will start to lose energy. That's why every 90 days you need to revisit those goals and re-energise yourself for the next quarter. 90 days is also 1% of 25 years, so each quarter needs to be a 1% step towards your lifetime goals.

The secret to having a great system is not to just to have lifetime goals and 90-day goals, but also to have several stops in-between. Starting with your lifetime goals is fantastic, but you then need to work backwards. In order to hit your lifetime goals, ask what you need to achieve in the next 3 years to be on track. In order to do these, what do you need to do this year? In order to achieve this year's goals, what do you need to achieve this quarter? In order to achieve these quarterly goals, what do you need to do this month, and for these monthly goals, what do you have to do this week? Oh, and by the way, you need these for each of your roles!

This sounds like a lot of work, and it is if you don't have a system. That's why I want to share with you 'The Limitless Life Planner'- the secret to my success. It obviously requires more work at the start, but once created you can build on it. Rather than duplicate your efforts for this, and instead of giving you an exercise table, I'd rather you download 'The Limitless Life Planner' from **www.thetrusted.team/llp**. Once you have it, watch the explanation video of how to use it, and then book half a day in your diary to complete the 'Goals' tab.

Not only is The Limitless Life Planner a great tool for writing out your goals, it also ensures that you're working through a 'to do list', which you should refer to several times a day. The more you can see those goals, the more likely you are to achieve them. You will notice that on the 'Time' tab section of the explanation video, I say your 'to do list' should also display your quarterly and monthly goals. That way you can continually be reminded of what they are. Your 4-6 most important tasks are also there, staring you in the face each day. By having that constant reminder, you will achieve so much more.

One of the other benefits of The Limitless Life Planner is that it frees up your working memory. As a business owner you have loads of jobs, ideas and thoughts bouncing around in your head. Things you must remember to do, things you must remember to talk to your team about, and all this would ordinarily clog up your working memory. Not the working memory on your computer, but in your head. This causes unnecessary stress, as you are constantly worried about getting everything done, or that you've missed something.

On a computer, you have a hard disk and you have working memory called Random Access Memory known as RAM. The hard disk is where everything is stored, and the RAM is where the programs that you are currently working on sit. Have you noticed that as you open more programs, your computer starts to run more slowly? That is because your RAM is being clogged up with too many processes. It has too many things to think about and, as a result, it runs less efficiently. You can speed it up again, by closing down some of those programs that you aren't currently using. You brain works the same way. The more things you have whirring around in your brain, the more worried and the less focused you will be. That is why you too need a hard disk, and that is The Life Planner.

By using The Limitless Life Planner effectively, each time you have an idea or remember something that needs doing, you note it down, knowing that at the right time, you can come back to it, regardless of when you think of it. You can park it on your hard disk, The Limitless Life Planner, and then forget about it until it is the right time to address it. This will ensure you achieve so much more both because you'll never forget anything, and because you are free to focus your attention on what is important in that moment.

I also teach this exercise in more depth at the free Limitless Life Workshop. If you'd like to know more, please visit **www.thetrusted.team/the-limitless-life-workshop**

## Chapter Summary

- Build goals that are more in line with your life's objectives by defining your key roles in your business and personal life.
- Achieve more in less time by identifying ways to achieve two goals at once.
- Gain a better work life balance by implementing a time system and constructing 'The Happy Week'.
- Create a goal delivery system that ensures you consistently hit your targets using 'The Limitless Life Planner'.

# Section 3: The E.P.I.C. Business Blueprint

The 4-step guide to making more time in your business life.

| | |
|---|---|
| **E** | End Game |
| **P** | Plan |
| **I** | Innovate |
| **C** | Culture |

# Chapter 13: Innovate with Kaizen

*"There's a way to do it better—find it."* Thomas Edison

To truly generate entrepreneurial happiness, the time you spend at work has got to be fun and fulfilling. This comes from a number of areas, one of which is to delegate away everything you are either not very good at, or you don't enjoy, in the way we looked at in Chapter 10. A wise man once said, 'if you are not growing, you're dying', and that applies to your business. As we saw with the 6 Human Needs, as individuals we need to feel like we are growing, or getting better, to be genuinely happy. As an entrepreneur, the same applies in your business life. If you don't feel that your business is getting better than it was yesterday, you will never be happy at work.

At Tony Robbin's Business Mastery, he talked about the concept of the business lifecycle. This was compared to the lifecycle of a person.

At the beginning of your business' life, after its birth, the business is like a toddler. It doesn't really give you anything back, just some grief and the pride of ownership. It is a race for survival, and it needs 100% of your attention. It crashes around from one thing to another and causes as much chaos as it solves. The company is learning to walk.

As the company grows, money is tight, and it is very much a hand to mouth business. Cash-flow is the biggest restraining factor. That said, your people and your brand are growing. Your business is learning to run.

As a teenager, cash-flow is less of a problem, because the business is flying high, and you think you're a genius. Almost everything you touch turns to gold. Your business is making progress and you're making good sales, but not necessarily great profits. One of the biggest problems though is that it still requires the business owner to run the business and often to generate the revenue.

Teenagers also have a habit of taking too many risks. Some pay off, but some don't, and these risks can be the making or the breaking of your business. Because the business owner is still at the helm, there is also the risk that the lack of adequate management leads to the downfall of the business.

The next stage is the young adult. Those who don't take too many risks in the teenage years progress to making healthy sales with stronger cash-flow. That said, in the young adult stage you'll find the processes and systems are the areas that tend to hold it back. To progress, business owners need to make the systems more scalable and repeatable. It is also the stage where the business owner is starting to step back from some of their roles, delegating more. It is at this stage that the profits start to appear.

If you make it through the young adult stage, you can reach the mature adult stage. The prime of your life. At this stage, you have the systems in place to run the business smoothly. Strong growth can continue, but in a more sustainable fashion. The main characteristic here is that the business owner now has a management team in place, so that they are free to spend as little or as much time in the business as they choose.

It is at the mature adult stage that the business is worth the most. It is the most saleable, and this is essentially what we have been trying to move you towards through this book. Delegate to others, create amazing and repeatable systems, and have handsome profits to show for it. The company becomes much less dependent on the founder.

This sadly is not the end. From here, the company can continue to age, and reaches mid-life evaluation. Things begin to breakdown; the company loses its way a little as it continues to age. Old systems make it less and less dynamic.

From here, the business becomes an ageing business. Breakdown continues to accelerate like a Tesla in 'Ludicrous Mode': The problems in the business seem to be from external causes not internal, and you blame others for the short comings. Your most talented people start to leave.

The next stage is institutionalisation, where the organisation is only kept alive through outside help like subsidisation. Sadly, the stage after this is death.

Once the business progresses past mature adult, the stage at which the business is at its most valuable, and in it's prime, it is possible to return there. But the only way to do that is to innovate.

Let's take Apple as an example. After Steve Jobs was booted out of Apple in 1985, the company started to age. It came close to collapse, so was probably as far gone as institutionalisation. Steve Jobs returned to Apple in 1997 and, in order to save it, he simplified the range, eliminating many of the options that customers had because they caused complexity. He then ramped up the innovation of the company, leading to the introduction of the iMac, then the iPod, iTunes, the iPhone and then the iPad. It was through innovation that Steve brought Apple back from Institutionalisation, back to its prime.

Ironically, in the absence of Jobs, it could be argued that it has again crept back into mid-life evaluation again, and maybe even an aging company, as innovation has slowed. The introduction of the Apple Watch was less successful than expected and, at the point of writing, Apple shares are falling as a result of falls in iPhone sales. It has been knocked off the top spot of being the most valuable company in the world by Amazon, which by the way is constantly innovating. If Apple wants to return to its former glory, it needs to innovate.

If you want to ensure that your company continues to grow and improve, you must ensure that you are constantly innovating. To use the words of Tony Robbins, 'you need to strive for constant and never-ending improvement.'

## Marginal Gains

In his excellent book, 'Legacy', James Kerr looks at how Clive Woodward transformed the England team. When he took over management of the England team, they were, in Graham Henry's terms, 'world champions at wasting talent'. Clive Woodward started to look at every aspect of the game, to see how they could make small improvements that would amount to a lot.

According to Woodward, a team's success comes down to how a team work under pressure, how they understood teamwork and loyalty, and how they were able to 100 things just 1% better. This last piece was called the 'critical nonessentials'. Things like a fresh shirt at half time, a more inspiring locker room at Twickenham and the same bus for every game. All these small changes ultimately led to that infamous Jonny Wilkinson drop goal in injury time, which led to England winning the Rugby World Cup in 2003.

The same approach was taken by David Brailsford as headed up the British Cycling team as it prepared for the London 2012 Olympics. In an Olympics where they won an amazing 7 out of 10 gold medals, these marginal gains included customised aerodynamic helmets, hot pants worn between races to keep thigh muscles warm, sweat resistant clothing, alcohol sprayed on wheels at the start of the race to improve traction, and hypo allergenic pillows. In another excellent book 'Sleep: The Myth of 8 Hours' Nick Littlehales talks about how team Sky took this a stage further in the Tour de France. Not only did they select the right pillows, they selected the right beds, and after each day, they rolled them up, and took them onto the next hotel to ensure that every night the cyclists and their support team got the best night's sleep possible.

The idea is that, if you take each stage of the process you designed in 'The Phenomenal Process Producer' and improve it by 1%, you don't just get a 1% gain. If it is a 10-step process, you get a 10% gain. As you might remember, our process at Efficient Portfolio had 6-steps. It was actually many more when you look at what goes on behind the scenes, but as far as the client was concerned, there were 6 stages. For Efficient Portfolio, if we increased each stage's efficiency by 5%, it would have generated a 62% increase in our business.

In my 3 Steps to Entrepreneurial Happiness, I use an exercise called 'The Game of Gains'. This is about constantly evolving and innovating in every aspect of your business to ensure growth and vitality, something every business owner needs to integrate into their strategy.

The Game of Gains isn't just a strategy; it's a mindset. It revolves around the idea of constant innovation — not just big leaps, but small, consistent improvements in all areas of your business. This concept taps into our fundamental need for growth, recognized as one of the six human needs essential for fulfilment. When businesses stop growing, stagnation sets in, and it's usually the beginning of the end. As business owners, to keep our passion alive and our businesses thriving, we must foster an environment of continuous improvement and innovation.

To learn more about this concept and more, why not register for the free 3 Steps to Entrepreneurial Happiness workshop? **www.thetrusted.team/virtual-workshops**

## Innovate, Innovate and Innovate Some More
*"Formal education will make you a living; self-education will make you a fortune."* Jim Rohn

Once upon a time, in the land of innovation and industry, there was a renowned automaker named 'Toyota'. This company wasn't just known for its cars, but for its unique philosophy called 'Kaizen', which means 'continuous improvement.' Toyota believed that the journey to perfection wasn't a distant destination but a constant path of betterment, no matter how small the steps.

In the heart of Toyota's factories, everyone from the CEO to the assembly line workers practiced Kaizen. Each day, they were encouraged to find small ways to improve their work.

Whether it was arranging tools more efficiently, simplifying a step in the assembly process, or just tidying up the workspace, every little enhancement was celebrated. These tiny increments of change began to accumulate, leading to significant improvements in quality, efficiency, and employee morale. The Kaizen culture transformed Toyota into an industrial giant, admired across the globe for its dedication to excellence and its lean production system.

Meanwhile, far across the ocean, there was another automaker, 'General Motors' (GM). GM was facing tough times. Their factories were struggling, costs were high, and their cars were not selling as they once did. The once mighty titan of the automotive industry was in dire need of help.

In an unprecedented move, GM opened its doors to Toyota, seeking wisdom from the masters of efficiency. Together, they formed a joint venture, taking over a failing GM plant with the intention of turning its fortunes around using the principles of Kaizen.

This plant became known as 'NUMMI' (New United Motor Manufacturing, Inc.), a place where two cultures and philosophies would collide and eventually coalesce. The workers at NUMMI were skeptical at first, having been accustomed to a very different style of management. They were used to a top-down approach, where orders were given and followed without question, and where the whistle dictated the beginning and end of a grueling workday.

Toyota's team began to weave the Kaizen way into NUMMI's fabric. They introduced the idea that everyone had a voice and that the workers on the floor often had the best insight into how to improve the process they were a part of. They established systems where any worker could pull a cord and stop the production line if they spotted a problem, a stark contrast to GM's previous practice where halting the line was almost considered a taboo.

Days turned into weeks, weeks into months, and slowly, the plant began to transform. The employees started to take ownership of their work. They began to form teams and hold regular meetings to discuss how they could perform their tasks more efficiently. Ideas flowed, small changes were implemented, and the culture of continuous improvement took root.

The results were astonishing. Quality soared, productivity increased, and the same workers who had once toiled under the old regime were now the champions of change. The vehicles produced at NUMMI were ranked among the highest in quality, not just within GM's portfolio, but in the entire North American market.

The story of NUMMI became a legendary example of Kaizen in action. It showed how a philosophy that embraced small, daily improvements could rescue a failing factory and turn it into a bastion of industry-leading practices. Toyota's Kaizen had not just grown its own company, but it had also reached out across the world to help another, proving that the seeds of continuous improvement could indeed flourish in any soil, given time and commitment.

And so, the legacy of Kaizen continued, a testament to the belief that there's always room for improvement, no matter how successful one becomes.

So, how do you ensure that you constantly innovate?

At my former company, Efficient Portfolio, we generated Kaizen, or constant improvement by doing what we called at the time ENERGI meetings every month. I won't bore you with what It stands for, because over time none of us could remember, so it clearly wasn't important. That said, the concept was brilliant, and it ensured that we build a team with an intreprenurial mindset of constantly looking for ways to improve what we do.

Once a month, relevant members of the team met to work on improving the business. Some sessions were longer, and some shorter, but 90 minutes would be a typical session.

We had a series of meetings that we work on over the course of the year, and more got added as we saw processes and areas we needed to work on. These meetings were about 'working on' the business, not 'working in' it. They were about bringing the team together to all identify ways in which we could continue to improve as a business. Some involved working on the behind-the-scenes things, some the client facing work, some on the marketing, and others on our values. Each one had a specific purpose and was a great way for us to improve what we did as a team.

Today, we help the members of The Trusted Team generate Kaizen in their business through 'The Kaizen Constant'. This is a monthly meeting that they dial into with some or all of their team, and we coach them through a 90-minute brainstorming session, each on a different part of the business. Whether its cutting costs or creating better marketing, there are 12 Kaizen meetings we cycle through to ensure your business too benefits from constant Kaizen.

## Working ON the Business

*"The people who are crazy enough to think they can change the world are the ones who do."* Steve Jobs

In additional to doing it as a team, it is essential for the business owner to put aside time each quarter to 'work on the business' as opposed to 'working in the business'. Whilst I appreciate this is not the norm, it is the key to success for most successful businesses. Afterall, if you don't do it, you don't know if you are heading in the right direction.

When I first decided to get into triathlon, I had a lot to learn. I had spent the prior 3 years cycling more and more, setting my myself long and longer challenges. When I first bought a bike as an adult, I signed up to a 100-mile charity bike ride from Rutland to the Norfolk coast, in order to give me the motivation to use it. I ended up completing that charity ride, but I was the only rider out of around 500 that did it on a mountain bike. I was on a learning curve that was steeper than the Rutland hills. The following year I entered the London Surrey 100 mile, and successfully completed that. The year after that I entered The Dragon Ride, the 142-mile ride through both the Black Mountains and the Brecon Beacons in Wales. There were some serious climbs that day, and it was a tough challenge, but one I mastered all the same.

At the end of that year, when I was setting my goals for the year ahead, I needed something else, a new challenge. Should I find another ride that is longer and steeper or find something different? I'd just finished reading 'Finding Ultra' by Rich Roll. 'Finding Ultra' is a brilliant book about another 40ish year-old guy, right in the heart of midlife crisis territory, realising that he had seriously neglected himself. A school champion swimmer, he decided to try triathlons, and eventually became very good at them, to the point where he tried to complete seven Ironman Triathlons in seven days on seven different Hawaiian Islands. Spoiler alert: he did it, but it took him ten days not 7, due to the logistics of getting from one island to the next. What's even more incredible is that he did it with a guy who only had 1 arm!

I had just finished reading this and concluded that I wanted to give triathlons a try, and so, as I usually do, I set myself the 1-year goal of completing two sprint triathlons, one Olympic distance triathlon, and 1 half Ironman in the year ahead. I also sheepishly put a full Ironman into my 3-year goals, although I told no one! I hadn't ever run more than 6 miles before, so running a marathon going to be a challenge, and I hadn't swum more than a few lengths at any one time since leaving school, so that would be too.

As with anything I do, I went out to find the best people to help me I could. For the running, I read 'Born to Run' a fantastic book that I would recommend to any runner or wannabe runner. The story of the Tarahumara tribe, written by Christopher McDougall, an American journalist, is quite brilliant for 3 reasons: Firstly, it told the story of these incredible people who run almost barefoot over 100 miles per day as part of their tribal culture, just for fun, without ever getting injured. The story continues onto how another American known as 'Caballo Blanco', living in Mexico with the Tarahumara, brought some of America's top Ultra Runners down to compete against them.

Secondly, this book looks at the history of the human race, and how we, the Homo-Sapiens, survived but the

Neanderthals died out as a result of our running prowess allowing us to track down animals, and that we are literally, 'born to run'. Finally, it also provides a number of great suggestions on how to improve your technique to minimise injuries and maximise your speed. I regularly recommend this book to people wanting to get into running, and even better, I tell them to listen to it while running. I went from a person who had regularly said that 'running is like sport with all the fun bits removed,' to being hooked.

With regards to swimming, I realised a book wasn't going to cut it, so I found the best swimming coach with the best facilities in our area to give me some areas to improve. My coach used video analysis to coach me on how I was breathing at the wrong point in the swimming stroke, and how I needed to become more streamlined in the water.

Having got through the two sprint and one Olympic triathlons unscathed, The Vitruvian, my first half Ironman consisting of a 1900m swim, 85km bike and a 21km run, finally arrived. This was my big challenge for the year, and I was determined to complete it. I thought the swim went fairly well and was enthusiastic getting onto the bike. As I left transition I got into the flow, and then turned on my Garmin. As I was looking at the Garmin not the road, I hit a speed bump and was sent flying. Blood dripping from my leg and elbow, I shook myself down, decided nothing on me or the bike was broken, and headed on. Omitting that slight incident, the race went according to plan, and I finished in bang on 6 hours. Not fast, but I had finished: A challenge that had seemed impossible just a few months earlier.

When I came to setting my goals for 2018, the following year, I concluded that my goal was to do the same events, but to take off 5% off my times. Should I just train harder? It would have been very easy to say that I just need to run more and further, cycle longer and swim more. That would work to a certain extent, but would it be enough, and if not, what was my alternative? Should I train smarter rather than harder? Work on my technique not just my fitness? I decided that time was already fairly stretched between work and family, and whilst I would train harder, I would definitely need to train smarter.

I started to analyse my work outs. My swim worried me, as it had taken me 31 minutes to swim 1.5km and then 48 minutes to swim the 1.9km, so I started looking more closely at it. I realised that after more detailed analysis, I hadn't actually swum 1.5km and 1.9km, I had swum over 10% more in both instances. On a swim that was supposed to be 1.5km, I had actually swum 1.8km. No wonder I was slow, I was swimming way further than I needed to. On my swim to the buoy, when looking at the map, I had veered all-over the place, and that added unnecessary distance to my swim.

On the bike, I looked at my bike set up compared to others. I had a bike built for comfort on long rides, but everyone else had time trial bars on their bike, making them far more aero dynamic, plus fancy helmets that made them look like Sir Chris Hoy in the velodrome. On the run, I knew I had suffered from cramps, so I needed to research my nutrition, fluids and electrolytes to eliminate that risk.

So, what did I do? I read books on swim technique, particularly around swimming in a straighter line; after all, one of the easiest ways to increase your swim speed is to cut the distance you swim! I changed my swimming stroke so that I breathed on both sides as opposed to the same side, and I practiced sighting, the concept of looking up during your stroke to see your target. With regards to the bike, I invested in the right equipment to allow me to cut through the air much more easily. Finally, on the run, I read about nutrition and hydration to find ways to eliminate the cramp risk.

When it came to The Vitruvian, 1 year later, I felt hopefully I could get my time down from 6 hours to 5.43, which was the 5% reduction in my annual goals. What I did, amazed even me.

On the day of the race, I told my family to get there expecting a 5.30 finish, as I thought there was zero chance I would be any better than that. We have an ongoing joke about the fact that they missed me at the finish of pretty much all of my previous challenges, for one reason or another, so they didn't want to miss this one.

But they still did. I came sailing in after 5.15, a whopping 45 minutes quicker than the previous year, and way faster than I could have possibly hoped for. Not fast in some people's eyes of course, but for me that was quick. Why did this happen though?

The reason I managed to knock 45 minutes off my previous years' time, was because I chose to work on my approach, rather than just doing more training. My technique changes to my swimming reduced my swim distance, and that improved my speed, saving me a whopping 12% of my time. My changes to the bike and run each saved me around 5% on my previous time. Knowing what I know now, this could have been even more.

The point is that I was working **on** the business of training, as well as working **in** the business of training, and you need to do the same with your business. I was reading books, seeking the advice of other people with more experience than I, and researching ways to improve the equipment I used. It would have been easier just to carry on running, cycling and swimming, in the hope that I got better, but it wouldn't have achieved the same results.

Since that day, I've gone on to complete many full Ironmans that involve a 2.4-mile swim, a 112-mile bike ride and a 26.2-mile marathon run. My times have varied from 12 hours 12 minutes down to 10 hours 39 minutes as I've continued to apply this approach, totally exceeding what I thought was possible.

In business, it is so easy to get bogged down with clients' queries, emails and a never-ending to-do list, and that stops you improving the way you work. As a result, it is vital that you put time aside to work on the business. To look above the waterline and to see where you are going. After all, you may not be heading towards the buoy, you may be following another competitor out into open sea!

I make a point of always working at least 1 day a quarter <u>on</u> the business. In reality, as the business grows, 1 day a quarter isn't anywhere near enough. That could be on a specific course, like we provide at The Trusted Team, but it can also be me locking myself in a room with a series of exercises to go through over the course of a day. That said, I've found that approach to be more difficult and less effective.

It used to be that I did this by myself, and I didn't get any of my team to take the same approach. After a helpful suggestion from a friend, I realised that we should be getting them to do this too. As a result, I now insist that everyone in the team spends a minimum of 1 hour per month working on the business. This isn't their time at the ENERGI meeting, but this is time at their desk when they have to down tools, stop working, and start thinking about how we could run our business better. That can be ways to improve the element of the business they work in, but it can also be ideas for areas of the business that they aren't even involved in.

It is limited to 1 page of A4, so that it doesn't take too long to go through the whole teams' ideas, but it has a number of benefits. Firstly, they feel valued, as you are asking them for their opinion. Secondly, over the course of the month they are actively looking for ideas as to how we can improve the business, so that they have something to write about. It is a great way for new employees to give ideas that they see when they are new to the business; before they become indoctrinated into your processes. Finally, you can set themes, so one month it might be ways to create a better office environment, or ways to become more eco-friendly.

I'd encourage you to build structure around how you and your team spend time working on the business, to ensure you are getting to the finish line as quickly and efficiently as you possible can.

## Learning Library
*"Give me six hours to chop down a tree and I will spend the first four sharpening the axe."* Abraham Lincoln

Jim Rohn once said, "If you want a guaranteed strategy to become wealthy beyond your dreams, 25 years from now, all you need to do is read 1 book per week." I couldn't agree more.

By now, you should have worked out that I read a lot of books. If I want to improve an area of my life or my business, I try and find the best books to read, and then I action what I learn. A few years ago, I was reading a book called 'Delivering Happiness' by Tony Hsieh, the founder of Zappos, the online shoe retailer in the US that sold to Amazon for $1.2bn. I can't even remember what Zappos were doing at the time that gave me this idea, maybe exactly as we now do, but it was an idea that has had a huge impact on our business.

I have found huge value in reading different books. As you saw in the last chapter, just with regards to triathlons they first inspired me, they turned running from a chore into a joy, and they helped me swim in a straighter line. In business, they given me endless ideas as to how we can run our companies better and more effectively. Personally, books like Tony Robbin's Awaken the Giant Within have had a huge impact on my approach to life, my happiness and my health.

What 'Delivering Happiness' suggested was that I encourage my team to do the same. In fact, I concluded, not only would I encourage them to read these books, I was so confident that they would help improve them as both people and employees, I promised to pay them more. I will never forget the day I came back from that holiday and told the team about that idea. I remember Charlotte, now my longest standing employee saying; "Did I hear you right, you are going to pay us more to read books? Count me in!"

We created a structure that gave people a scale to ascend using title's like 'The Wizard' and 'The Guru', and for every 5 books they read in the Learning Library, our little library of the books I had read that I thought would be valuable, we'd pay the team more.

Over the years, the team have read many of the top books that I have read, and, as a result, they have grown more than I could have possibly hoped. They have learnt so much quicker than I did, because they were often given the tools earlier than I had found them.

What it also does is sieves out the sponges from the rocks. In life, you meet some people who know it all, and don't want to learn or improve themselves. These are your rocks. You also meet others who want to be the best they can be, by learning as much as possible. These are your sponges. In my experience, you will have a much stronger, dynamic business if you have a team full of sponges. When you breed a culture of growth, a culture I'll talk more about in the next chapter, you need to find ways to identify the gems. Overtime, hang onto the sponges, discard the rocks and your business will be far stronger for it. The Learning Library concept helps you find out who is a rock and who is a sponge.

The Learning Library also ties in really nicely with the concept of their 'Working on the Business'. Once a team member has finished a book, the theme for their Working on the Business should be around what they have learned from that book that could be used to improve our business.

I can't tell you how invigorating it is as a business owner to have your team regularly reading insightful business and personal development books and coming up with a flurry of new ideas. What better way to create a dynamic and motivated team than to have them learning and growing on the job?

I regularly get asked for book recommendations from people, inside our team and out, so you can find my top 12 business book recommendations and more at **www.thetrusted.team/life-library**

As long as you take action with what you read, it will transform your business. After all, 'growth' is one of our human needs, and if you are not growing you are drying. To put it another way, in the words of Ray Kroc, 'When you are green you are growing, when you are ripe you rot!'

## Unilever's Nozzle

When it comes to innovating in your business, you can get caught up working out how best to do something. As I already mentioned, procrastination is a fear of starting, so it is often better to get on and try, but sometimes you need more than that.

In the book 'Blackbox Thinking' by Matthew Syed, he looks at the story of Unilever, which I told you about earlier in this chapter. There are two morals to this story: Firstly, the importance of innovation; but secondly about not fearing mistakes through trial and error.

You need to apply this approach to your marketing, and to your business in general. You may not have any idea what the best solution or strategy is, but try as many different variations as you can, and as long as you measure the results, and act based on those measurements, you can evolve a business process, solve a business problem, or build an incredible marketing machine.

For example, with your marketing, rather than doing a single advert on Facebook, do three, or even better, ten. Identify the one that converts the best, and then create and test different variations of that. Do this again and again, and eventually you'll have an amazing marketing machine that you originally had no idea about.

Tying in with this is an approach is an idea that comes from another book from my top 12 list, 'The Lean Start-up' by Eric Ries. This is a book has one relatively simple principle: Do not get caught up with trying to create perfect. Create something that works, get it out there, and evolve from there.

If you try and build the perfect business you'll spend a lot of your time building stuff that turns out to be unimportant. Much better is to get a basic version of whatever you need out there, get people's feedback, and work on the bits that they will appreciate.

For example, if you are setting up a new business, don't get too caught up with having fancy business cards, an all singing and all dancing website, the perfect logo or any gimmicks. Work out what the Minimum Viable Product (MVP) is, and only build that. For some businesses, that may simply be persuading someone to part with their cash for a service you are going to deliver.

The benefit of doing this is that you get to prove the concept first. You also can then get paid to build the rest of the concept, whilst making sure you build the bits that are most important to you. This approach even works for the big tech companies like Microsoft and Apple. When they release a new product, it is often fraught with problems and bugs. By essentially asking their audience to be their guinea pigs, you'd think they'd alienate their customers, but actually it turns them into raving fans.

For me, the best example of this is Tesla. I love my Tesla Model S. Not only is it a step towards ridding the world of fossil fuels and introducing the future of driverless cars, the vehicles are also constantly getting better and better. I often get into my car first thing in the morning to find out that there has been a software update, and my car just got better. This could be something serious, like improving the functionality of the autopilot feature, or it could be something less serious like the recent addition of Emission Testing Mode, which essentially creates a whoopy cushion on one of the seats in the car, so that when you indicate, varying degrees of flatulence noises come out of the corner of the car's speaker!

Whilst you could legitimately argue that adding farting sounds to the functionality hasn't improved the car, or altered its value, the same could not be said about the improved Autopilot. My children would probably tell you the opposite however! When I come to sell my car, I might be selling 3-year-old hardware, of which there are only 35 moving parts, but I will also be selling brand new software and features. The car is evolving with me and with the technology available, and I love it as a result. Like a fine wine, it is maturing with age.

Speaking of Tesla, in the world of advanced automotive technology, Tesla has been a front-runner, particularly with its development of the Autopilot system. This system, a shining example of machine learning and artificial intelligence in action, enables Tesla vehicles to navigate complex driving scenarios with increasing competence over time. One remarkable instance that underscores the potential of Tesla's Autopilot occurred with a particularly challenging corner on a twisty road. A Tesla encountered this corner and, like any learner, initially struggled to handle it smoothly. However, this wasn't a setback but an opportunity for growth. Thanks to the car's sophisticated sensors and software, the car's experience wasn't just a momentary challenge; it was a valuable data point.

Here's where the magic of Tesla's collective learning comes into play. The car's data on how it managed the corner—its speed, steering angles, and braking—was anonymized and sent back to Tesla. There, engineers used this real-world data to refine the algorithms that guide the Autopilot's decision-making process. But the learning didn't stop with just that one car. Once improved, these algorithms were pushed out as an update to all Tesla vehicles on the road through an over-the-air software update. Suddenly, every Tesla around the world was equipped with the knowledge of how to approach that once-difficult corner, and any similar ones it might encounter, more adeptly.

This process exemplifies a revolutionary aspect of Tesla's approach: Collective learning. Each individual vehicle's experiences contribute to the collective intelligence of the entire fleet. As a result, a Tesla not only becomes smarter and more capable with every drive it takes but also makes every other Tesla smarter in turn. Thus, when a Tesla learned to navigate a challenging corner, it wasn't just an achievement for that vehicle alone. Every Tesla, existing or yet to roll off the production line, shared in that knowledge, making the entire fleet safer and more adept at handling the complexities of real-world driving. This story not only highlights the innovative spirit of Tesla but also paints a future where technology and teamwork merge to create a continuously improving driving experience.

Through systems like The Kaizen Constant and building Outstanding Operations, you can ensure that this principal can be strategically woven into your business. It also highlights another important point: the power of AI. AI was able to learn how to take that corner, to the extent where at some point it will be better than any human driver on the planet, even Lewis Hamilton!

AI is going change so much in our business, we need to ensure that we are embracing it in every aspect of our business. You probably won't lose your job or customers to AI just yet, but you will lose it to someone using AI, because they have the power of 10 people! That is why one of the modules we include and keep cycling back to in The Trusted Team is 'The AI Advance'. This ensures you are at the forefront of this development, which I have no doubt will be as big a change as the introduction of the internet was!

As with most things, you can achieve most of what you need to do with 80% of the finished product. The remaining 20% takes so long to finish off and is often what gives you the 'headache' of finishing a project. I'd argue that you should forget the last 20%, and get on and release at 80%, or even less if possible. The feedback that you get from doing so will reshape what your 100% looks like anyway, and this way you will save time and wasted effort. In any project, work out what your Minimum Viable Product is, and get on with rolling that out. Clearly do not put people at risk in doing do; if Tesla hadn't perfected the brakes, clearly, they shouldn't be releasing the car, but with the essentials covered, get it out there for the world to see. It may transform your end goal.

Learning, attending courses and reading is a way of evolving yourself. We don't quite know where we will end up as a result, but if we don't go through the process, one thing is for sure, and that is you won't evolve into anything better.

In my Better Future Framework, I get people to do an exercise to help them work on what that should look like. You can find out more about this at **www.thetrusted.team/BFF**.

## Chapter Summary

- Improve what you do in your business by using regular ENERGI meetings with your team to 'work on the business'.
- These can help you refine your customer facing processes, your back-office processes and turn you into a business of constant and never-ending improvement.
- See massive gains in what you achieve by finding ways to make small improvements in every step of your client journey through the 10 x 10 x 10 meeting.
- Avoid aging as a business by looking at ways you can constantly innovate your way to success.

- Fail fast through 'Blackbox Thinking' so that through a process of elimination you can nail down the most successful strategy for the best results.
- Create a motivated and loyal team through constant and ongoing learning. Encourage your team to read new books by initiating a Learning Library in your business.

# Chapter 14: Grow Your Culture

*"To make customers happy, we have to make sure our employees are happy first."* Tony Hsieh, Zappos

'Why did your product or company fail?' When posed with this question, people always give you a permutation of the same three things: Undercapitalised; the wrong people; and bad market conditions. It's always the same three things. So, let's explore that.

I am guessing that you have probably heard of the Wright Brothers- the first men to pilot an airplane. I don't want to tell you about them though, I want to tell you a story that features in the book 'Start with Why', by Simon Sinek. It's a story about Samuel Pierpont Langley. Most people don't know about Samuel Pierpont Langley, but he was important back in the late 19th century, when the race was on to be the first to successfully build a motorised aeroplane and fly it with a pilot. During this exciting time of innovation, Samuel Pierpont Langley had what you would assume to be the recipe for success.

Samuel Pierpont Langley was given $50,000 by the War Department to figure out the puzzle of this flying machine. Given this was the 1890s, this was a substantial amount of money, so capital wasn't the problem. He held a seat at Harvard and worked at the Smithsonian and was extremely well connected, recruiting the help of some of the best minds of the day for the project, including Dale Carnegie. The market conditions were also fantastic. The New York Times followed him around everywhere and everyone was rooting for Langley, so the country was right behind him in their support. Then how come most people have never heard of Samuel Pierpont Langley?

A few hundred miles away in Dayton, Ohio, lived Orville and Wilbur Wright. They had none of what we consider to be the recipe for success. They had no money; they paid for their dream with the proceeds from their bicycle shop. Not a single person on the Wright brothers' team had a college education. Not even Orville or Wilbur. And the New York Times hadn't heard of them. So how did two unknown brothers make history? The difference was that Orville and Wilbur were driven by a cause, a purpose, a belief. They believed that if they could figure out this flying machine, it would change the course of the world.

With a purpose you will find a drive, and ultimately reward and fulfilment, which leads to becoming a recipe for success in many cases throughout history. If you can harness just a small amount of that for yourself and your team, you will make a formidable opponent.

In my first book, 'The Dream Retirement', I say "If you want to create a happy retirement, you need enough money to be able to sleep at night, enough purpose to get you up in the morning, and the health to allow you to do so." People in retirement often lose their purpose, because it is very often linked to their job, so they need to put effort into creating a new purpose.

That said, many people in work have no purpose, which is why so many people are unhappy. According to Arnold Schwarzenegger, in his motivational speech that broke the internet, 74% of Americans hate their job. Apparently in the UK it is around 55%, if the CV Library study is to be believed.

That means that most people spend most of their time doing something they hate. No wonder depression is on the rise.

Clearly defining what your business' purpose is helps you all know why you are doing what you are doing. It comes back to what I talked about in Chapter 4, and it may well be the same as your 'why statement', but you must keep reiterating this with your team. Not only that, ideally they should help you create it, so that they buy into it too. If your team truly believe in what you are doing as a business, and if they can see how you genuinely help people, they will buy into the company purpose, and that will bring you a much stronger and more passionate team.

In addition to your team knowing why they do what they do, they should also know why you go about your business in the way you do. This will help define what it means to be part of your team. This is called your company culture.

The reason Tony Hseih's book 'Delivering Happiness' is so powerful, is because it allows you to see the impact of creating a fantastic company culture. At Zappos they wanted to be known as delivering the best customer service of any company out there. They wanted people to talk about how amazing they were as a result of their experience of dealing with them.

In order to achieve this, when you phoned into Zappos, your customer services manager was tasked with helping you as much as possible. Hseih was so confident of his company's culture and the service they provided, he put it to the test in front of his closest friends. After a night out drinking, Tony and his pals tried to order pizza from their hotel at 2am, but they were informed that room service was now finished. Tony suggested that his friend phone Zappos customer services, to see if they could help.

Now please remember, Zappos are a shoe retailer, not a concierge service. But whilst the Zappos customer service couldn't deliver a pizza, they did track down a company that could, and placed the order for Tony's friend. Not bad customer service at all!

Why do you think that Zappos customer service department went so far above and beyond? It's because it is part of their company culture. Zappos are so confident of their culture in fact, after a new employee has worked for them for 1 month, they are offered $1000 to leave. Zappos know that for those who do, they were not the right fit for the business. This simply brings forward the decision to let them go and saves the company and the employee time and grief.

After reading this book, I was full of enthusiasm to implement Tony's advice and to build our company culture. In the book Hsieh said that it was vital we built it together as a team, rather than me tell everyone what the culture was, and now I understand why.

Within days of defining our company culture, I could sense a difference in the business. It was as if everyone was walking around the office with their shoulders pulled back just a little more than a few days earlier. They were standing taller, and they were acting with more pride. They had more purpose, and they were working better as a result.

What does it mean to be part of your business? Do you know? You might think you know, but is that what your employees think, because that might be very different. Will a new employee fit in with your current team and the ethos of the business? These are all questions that can be answered by building a company culture.

We review our company culture every year, as you saw when I talked about our Kaizen Meetings. That is one of the Kaizen Meeting topics, so once a year we spend time talking about it and refining it. That said, it hasn't really changed much since we first created it, which makes me feel it is pretty close to the mark. Whilst it was originally created for Efficient Portfolio, the company culture we follow has transcended to all of my businesses.

Here is our current company culture, which we call The EP Code.

| E | Embrace fun and be a little quirky |
| P | Pursue growth and learning |
| C | Constant and never-ending improvement |
| O | Open and honest relationships |
| D | Deliver' WOW' through client service |
| E | Energised, positive & passionate team |

We have this on our walls, we have it in our Team Planner document that we review weekly together, and we have it in our 'Culture Book'. Another idea I stole off Zappos, which I love.

Once a year we produce a hardback photobook of what it means to be part of the business. There are quotes from the team, an explanation of each point of The EP Code, and our values. This book is a wonderful record of what the business looked like years ago, but it is also a fantastic thing to have in your company reception for people to look at. What better way to tell your new prospects about your business and the culture within it?

Having now witnessed its impact for a number of years, I believe that having a company culture has a similar effect. Essentially you are programming into the minds of your team how they need to act to be part of the team. As long as that is good for them, as well as you, that has got to be a fantastic thing.

Finally, in-case you didn't now have enough reasons to document a company culture, here's one more. If you want to recruit as well as Google do, you need to know your company culture. Google base their interview process around their company culture, and so in recent years, we have done the same. We tell candidates what our culture is and ask them to give examples of how they have exhibited these qualities in the workplace.

This does 2 things: Firstly, those who genuinely fit your culture will be excited. This will not only be evident in the interview process but means that they will go home and decide that they really want to work for you. After all, you have to sell this job to them as well as they sell themselves to you. Secondly, from their answers you'll get a feel for whether they are likely to actually fit your culture. In my experience, it is the people who don't fit the company culture who end up causing you the most grief, even if they are brilliant at their role. It is good to spot this early on and save everyone a lot of pain and disruption. Once you have a company culture documented, build your recruitment process around it.

It also makes sense to look at this retrospectively too. Look at your current team and assess them against each of your culture traits. You may be surprised by what you see. It may well be that this process highlights something that in your gut you already knew. The one or two team members who just don't seem to fit in will become obvious. For everyone's benefit, you'll probably find that they are better served by working elsewhere.

I encourage you so put aside at least a couple of hours to put together your company culture. As a team, brainstorm what you think it means to be part of your company; pick the best ones and create something amazing from them. With company culture, you can grow something incredible!

At the Trusted Team we use 'The Culture Cultivator' to collate and develop these ideas. In today's fast-paced and ever-evolving business environment, having a strong, adaptable culture isn't just nice to have—it's essential. It's what differentiates the great from the good. The Culture Cultivator helps us to create businesses that are efficient and profitable, but also places where people feel valued, connected, and motivated to bring their best selves to work every day.

Remember, a strong company culture not only improves engagement and retention but also boosts productivity and ultimately, profitability. Let's cultivate a culture that empowers, inspires, and transforms. Let's build businesses where culture is the cornerstone of success.

## Code of Honour

In Legacy by James Kerr, which I mentioned earlier in this book, he talks a lot about the culture of the most successful rugby team of all time, the All-Blacks. In the All-Blacks team, they appoint a leadership team, which I will come back to in the next chapter. This is made up of the most senior, most capped and most respected 4 players of the moment: The likes of Dan Carter one of the best fly-halves of all time; Richie McCaw winner of an incredible 148 caps; and Tana Umaga, the first New Zealander of Pacific Island heritage to captain the All-Blacks, were all were part of this leadership team over the years.

Under Graham Henry in particular, the All-Blacks had a strong culture, and one of the rituals was known as 'sweeping the sheds'. After a game, and after the post-match briefing, all but the leadership team would leave the dressing room. The leadership team would then proceed to sweep the changing room, as an act to show that nothing was below even the top players.

Whilst this fits into a culture, this is also about how you act with your teammates. It's part of having a code of honour between you. Having a rule book that the team plays by. The company culture is about how we conduct our self as a business. A code of honour is more about how we act towards our fellow team members.

A number of years ago, we put together our Code of Honour, and again through our ENERGI meetings over the years we have refined it to the following:

**We praise more than we criticise**

**We never leave a team member behind.**

**We are always punctual, professional & prudent**

**We look forward not back**

**We treat others how we want to be treated**

**We don't make excuses; we find solutions**

On a number of occasions, as inevitably happens when employing a team, people have overstepped the mark, or have been letting their team members down. The Code of Honour allows you to easy highlight why there is a problem. You can even make their Code of Honour performance part of their bonus structure if you so wish, as we have done a couple of times. It's essentially a way of saying, 'are you playing as part of the team'? If they aren't, it allows that team member to consider why they are not hitting the mark.

As a business owner, a Code of Honour isn't something you should just create and inflict on your team. You need to work on it together, as it will have far more power and meaning, as everyone will take ownership of it. So, create a Code of Honour, and then incentivise people to stick to it!

## The Moonshot
*"Moonshot thinking starts with picking a big problem: something huge, long existing, or on a global scale."* Astro Teller

I first heard the term 'Moonshot' from Peter Diamandis, who I'll talk more about in the next chapter; however, I believe it actually originates as a term used by Astro Teller, who is the CEO of X (formerly Google X). Most entrepreneurs out there are trying to grow their business by 10%. Astro is focused on looking at growing the business by 10 times, which is quite a massive difference!

If you want to grow your business by 10 times, you need to think differently. You need a completely different mindset, and that is achieved by creating a 'Moonshot'.

In May 1961, President John F. Kennedy announced the almost insane goal of putting a man on the Moon by the end of the decade. The technology wasn't even close to being ready to achieve this. Nobody knew how it could happen, and yet this first 'Moonshot' was achieved just eight years' later. It was a huge goal, but as a result, people had to think very differently.

Steve Job's greatest trait was probably that he could see things that his customers didn't even know they wanted or needed. 'A thousand songs in your pocket' was a pipedream so far from what we had been used to, we didn't know we needed or wanted it, and yet now it is an essential part of life for most people. The smartphone even more so. The iPad, unbelievably successful, was just another example of 10x thinking, as when Jobs came up with the concept, the technology just wasn't there to make it possible. But with that in mind, he forced it through as soon as it was feasible.

If you want to grow your business, you need a Moonshot. If you want a culture in your business where everyone is pulling towards that growth, again you need a Moonshot!

At Efficient Portfolio our Moonshot was 'To help 1 million people through financial planning'. At the time we set this, if you had taken every Financial Planner in the UK, combined they could not cope with delivering financial planning to 1 million people. I genuinely had no idea how I could make this happen; however, I did know it would eventually be possible.

The universe has a habit of showing you the way, you just have to tell it what you want. A Moonshot is a simple way of communicating this mind-blowing goal to your team, to your subconscious, and to the outside world.

Again, decide on this with your team. Clearly as the entrepreneur you will have a strong sway on this one, but they do need to buy into it, otherwise you will be trying to do a Moon landing all by yourself!

We use 'The Moonshot Mindset' at The Trusted Team to help businesses set their own ultimate goals. "

The 'Moonshot' mindset is about setting audacious, seemingly unreachable goals—just like JFK did when he challenged NASA to make a moon landing happen within a decade. This concept got a modern twist in the business realm by Astro Teller at Google X, where they aimed not just for a 10% improvement, but for a 10X leap forward.

Imagine the transformation when you shift your thinking from making incremental gains to achieving exponential growth. By adopting a Moonshot mentality, you set yourself apart. Approach every challenge with the belief that it's solvable, even if the solution isn't immediately clear. This shift in mindset isn't just about thinking bigger—it's about thinking differently. It's the Moonshot Mindset that will redefine your business strategy and turbocharge your success, pushing you far beyond the ordinary.

If you'd like help crafting your own, please book in for a free coaching call with me by emailing **hello@thetrusted.team**

## Chapter Summary

- Build a better business by determining what it means to be a part of your business.
- By understanding what the culture of your business is, you can work better together, recruit better people and understand more clearly when someone doesn't fit into your team.
- Have a stronger team by creating a code of honour, so that you all treat each other with the respect that you and they would expect.
- Have your whole team driving towards a bigger, better future by having a clearly defined 'Moonshot'.

# Chapter 15: Prior Planning Prevents…..

*"If you don't know where you are going, you'll end up someplace else."* Yogi Berra

Caryl and I are a big fan of eating out. Over the years we have been fortunate enough to have eaten at some amazing national and international Michelin-starred restaurants. Many of these restaurants have been brilliant; but some have been distinctly underwhelming. Over time, if I am honest, the novelty has worn off, because we find that too many are of a similar ilk and just don't stand out.

Don't get me wrong, the food is lovely, and at the time you enjoy the occasion, but very few are truly memorable life experiences. However, one that does not fall into that category was 'The Fat Duck', Heston Blumenthal's restaurant in Bray. For as long as I live, I will not forget that evening.

Set in the heart of the Berkshire countryside, this village is unbelievably home to not one, but two Michelin Star restaurants: The 'Fat Duck' owned by Heston Blumenthal and Alain Roux's 'The Waterside Inn' (which we were fortunate enough to experience when we took the team away to celebrate the sale of Efficient Portfolio).

With The Fat Duck, what made this such a special experience was prior planning- by them and by us. This was a special place to eat, and very difficult to get a table, so we had waited until Caryl's 40th to treat ourselves and two sets of friends, the Olivers and the Wadas.

The prior planning by us involved making sure that 3-months to the day before we wanted to dine, we were online securing a table the second they went live. If you don't, you miss out. We booked ourselves into a hotel that was just a short taxi ride away. We planned the evening: Meet at the hotel bar for some champagne, followed by cocktails in another local pub called 'The Crown', then onto the Fat Duck for a memorable evening, and all topped off by Sunday lunch in 'The Hinds Head', Heston's pub in Bray, the following day.

The prior preparation by the team at 'The Fat Duck' was much more detailed. Already awarded 'The best restaurant in the world award' in 2008, 2009 and 2010, they didn't want to rest on their laurels, so in 2015 they closed for 6 months while they completely redesigned most of their menu. How many restaurants take their menu that seriously they are willing to completely close to work on it? Very few.

We were lucky enough to be joining them in May 2016, so not long into their new menu was launched. According to the critics, their prior planning had paid off, as the food and experience was apparently even better than before. When we booked the table, we had to pay for everyone's food upfront. The only time I have had to do that! More prior planning.

As the organiser, soon after booking I received an email from the restaurant. Nothing unusual there I thought, until I opened it. I was being sent on a journey and was asked to answer a number of questions about each of the guests: Which football team they supported, their business interests, etc. All of this sounded irrelevant to me at this stage, but soon all would become clear.

Now, I do not want to give away the magic of the experience in case you ever decide to visit yourself. It would be such a shame to spoil the surprise, so all I can really say is that we were blown away. By the 5$^{th}$ of 17 courses we'd already run out of superlatives. At different stages of the meal we had guests in tears- tears of joy as they were overwhelmed by the food and the experience.

Planning that meal to the finest of details took us on a journey that created the most wonderful of experiences. Whilst the food was amazing, it was only part of it. It was the show, the theatre, and ultimately, the preparation, that allowed the team at 'The Fat Duck' to deliver a night none of us will ever forget. It is all in the planning, and the same applies to your business.

## The Leadership Team

*"All change is hard at first, messy in the middle and gorgeous at the end."* Robin Sharma

In Chapter 12 I talked about 'The Limitless Life Planner'. This is about planning a better future by making commitments to yourself of the things you will achieve. The amazing thing about the Limitless Life Planner is that when you break your life up into 3-month periods, you can achieve so much more. 3 months just seems to be the right frequency. Any more frequent, and you give it less attention, do it less thoroughly, and you create fewer inspiring commitments and fall off the wagon.

Whilst on Dan Sullivan's Strategic Coach® I was writing out my own goals every quarter, and even when I had a break from attending the workshops, I continued to do this. I revamped how I structured my goals with the help of work from people like Brian Tracy and Tony Robbins, and I created a structure that worked really well for me. Originally these were all bunched together, but with the help of Tony Robbins, as you've now seen, they were broken up into personal goals and business goals, and even separated out into the different roles I play in my life.

That said, it was reading 'Traction', by Gino Wickman than made me look at this from a new business perspective. There was me setting my own personal and business goals every quarter, and also helping the team set theirs, but were we setting business goals as a team? We did set targets, but we weren't setting more specific goals.

As a result of reading Traction, I created 'The Leadership Team'.

Again, referring to 'Legacy', when the likes of Richie McCall and Graham Henry were about to pass the responsibility of the All Blacks leadership onto the players and coaches that would follow them, they needed to ensure that the leadership and systems that they had brought to the team could be continued. This is what witnessed too in Efficient Portfolio. By appointing my leadership team, I gave some of my key team members the responsibility and authority, which I had formerly held, to lead elements of my business, and the results paid dividends.

As soon as I created the leadership team, I saw a massive step up in how these guys and girls acted inside the business. How they dealt with problems, and how they moved the business forward, because they understood and are bought into the company's goals much more than ever before. So how did we achieve that?

Nowadays, in all of my businesses, my leadership teams meet every quarter, for a full day. Ideally this needs to be outside of the office. At the bare minimum, we need to be locked away in a meeting room undisturbed for the whole day, also stepping out for lunch, so there is no temptation to check our emails. The Agenda, which is derived from Gino Wickman's in Traction can be downloaded from here **www.thetrusted.team/tools**

You will see that I mention here 'The 1 Page Business Plan' a few times. This is our adaption of so many other things, and where we bring a lot of what we do together. You can download a copy of it on the same page too.

The 1 Page Business Plan covers our Core Values, 'The EP Code', our 'Why Statement' and our 'Moonshot'. This means that each quarter, as a minimum, the Leadership Team are revisiting and rereading what these are. That doesn't mean we tweak them each quarter, far from it, but it is acting as a reminder as to what we are trying to achieve, and how we are going to get there. The document also covers a summary of our marketing strategy for the year, our ten-year targets and what makes us unique. Finally, and most importantly for the purpose of the leadership meetings, it covers our goals: 3-year, 1 year and quarterly, plus our issues that need solving for that quarter.

The first part of the leadership meeting is spent reviewing what's working and what's not, how we got on achieving last quarter's goals, and what issues have cropped up in the business. The second part of the meeting is then about identifying the goals for the next quarter, some of which will have rolled over from the previous quarter. The next part of the day is about going through the issues in order of importance and working out solutions and strategies for each. For each solution, we add this to the goals for the quarter.

Finally, we assign each element of the goals between the leadership team members. That doesn't mean they have to do them themselves, but it does mean they are responsible for making sure they are done.

By taking this approach, I have a far more organised team, a better business and more free time too! My leadership team knows what page we are on, and they are pulling in the same direction as me. By having clearly defined goals for the business, over the next quarter, year and 3 years, they know the bigger picture, so they can make the right judgements with that in mind.

You may wonder, as I did, whether there would be enough to talk about for a whole day. We have never failed to fill the time. In 'Traction', Gino Wickman suggests that you also have an annual meeting (ideally at the end of the year) that is conducted over two days. For this meeting, the agenda continually evolves, and again the latest version can be found at **www.thetrusted.team/tools**

Essentially this is the same as the quarterly meeting with a few extra additions. As it is the annual meeting, in addition to reviewing your quarterly goals, you need to revisit and revamp and visualise your 3-year goals and you need to create new 1-year goals. You also need to do conduct a SWOT analysis, and I like to do a summary of a book I have read too.

I encourage you to create your Leadership Team. What that looks like will depend on your own business. Build the 1-

Page Business Plan with them, and then meet each quarter so that it evolves with your ever-changing business. At the start you may need to put aside longer to get that done, especially if you have not done any of this before, but I promise that you will not be disappointed with the results.

If you want some guidance on doing this, or you want to read more about how you can take this to the next level, I encourage you to book your free coaching call with me. It really is a fantastic business book and I'm happy to share my ideas and the ways in which I've implemented the strategies. If you then want further help implementing it, Gino Wickman has created a team of consultants around the world who will help you implement this and much more in your business.

Instill leadership into some key members of your team, and as a result, you will see an improvement across the entirety of the company. After all, when the tide rises, all ships rise too.

## The Brain Trust

Being a fan of Steve Jobs I was keen to read Ed Cutmull's book 'Creativity Inc', as Steve had such a huge impact at Pixar: He ploughed pretty much everything he had made from Apple into this studio. At times is seemed like this would backfire, but eventually it proved to be one of the best decisions he made. This is such a great business book, packed full of fascinating stories and wonderful ideas.

One of the most poignant stories in the book concerns the transformation of Monsters Inc. and how the original concept was reversed for the finished movie.

The early idea for this film was based on a man still dealing with the monsters who'd been hiding in his closet since childhood: Each monster would represent a particular unaddressed fear or trauma from the man's childhood, and as he found the courage to confront them in turn, they'd pack their things and move out.

After a lot of discussions with the Pixar team, that idea was flipped on its head, so the man became the monster and the object of his fears were the children. They redrafted the plot, switching the real and monster worlds around, but keeping its central premise intact: The mess and chaos of childhood intruding on an ordered adult life.

As a result of these changes, and many more, the initial film ideas were a million miles from what we know of the film today.

In another story, Catmull tells of how 'Toy Story 2' got deleted off the company's servers. This meant them losing 2 months' work and literally hundreds of hours just to get back to where they had already been.

Finally, there was the Pixar Atrium. When designing their new headquarters, Jobs wanted to create one central meeting place for the whole team. Even though it meant people walking further, he put mailboxes, toilets and the canteen in one central atrium. As a result, people were forced to bump into their colleagues more often, and that led to more conversations. This spurned more creativity and a better company culture. We have done the same at our HQ: The Hub and Spoke. Not quite as grand as Pixar's atrium by any stretch of the imagination, but by having a breakout area and a downstairs cafe we are trying to encourage those interactions between the team, because everyone benefits as a result. The Hub and Spoke is also a fantastic hub for local businesses to fuel, focus and connect with other like-minded entrepreneurs. It's also a cycling café at the weekends, so further connections can be made. To see more, please visit **www.thehubandspoke.co.uk**

One thing that struck me about Pixar, and some of it was definitely Jobs' influence, was that it was a forward-thinking company. One feature of their progressive nature was a weekly meeting called 'The Brain Trust'. Named after the key people that Franklin Roosevelt surrounded himself during his presidential administration, this was a meeting each Monday where Pixar thrashed out the week's issues.

At the time I introduced this, at Efficient Portfolio we were already meeting every Monday morning to talk about any issues in the business and also to make sure we all knew what the most important things each of us was doing that week. Calling it 'The Brain Trust' didn't change anything, other than the story behind it, thus the feel. Across my businesses, my teams now meet for The Brain Trust every Monday morning. It's always at the same time, which means we even have a voicemail set up that automatically tells people that's why we aren't answering at that time.

In this meeting, we always cover the following agenda, which can again be found at **www.thetrusted.team/tools**

Again, we start off with the best things that have happened that week. Always start meetings on a positive- it gets everyone into the right mindset and allows you to celebrate your successes.

Next, we talk about The Successful Business Scorecard, plus the business' quarters goals, so we can remind ourselves exactly what we are trying to hit and what we are all working towards. A communicated goal is 100% more likely to be followed through.

We then look at what is happening in the business for the week ahead, so we are all aware of any events or companywide meetings that are happening. Nothing worse than one of your team wandering in looking less smart than usual as 25 new prospective clients sit in reception waiting for a seminar!

That's followed by going through Team Planner, which is a crucial but simple tool we use to track people's accountability. Finally, something that I learned from The Strategic Coach® Program, is that we each list the 3 most important results we need to achieve that week. This is so that everyone knows what we need to do that week, so we all know where we stand and can collaborate on any overlapping projects.

It is a simple meeting, which usually lasts no more than 30 minutes, and keeps us all in tune with what is happening in the company. As the businesses have grown and diversified, it has helped us all remain close as a team. These weekly meetings are 'working in the business', but are then complemented by the monthly Kaizen Constant meetings where we are 'working on the business'.

I recommend you schedule in your own version of the Brain Trust meeting, once a week. We like Mondays, as it gets the team on track for the week ahead. Diarise your Brain Trust and help iron out the Monsters in your Inc!

## Chapter Summary

- Have a more saleable, better run and more dynamic business by creating a Leadership Team in your business.
- Nurture these leaders, so that can drive your business forward through quarterly structured leadership meetings.
- Generate more efficient teamwork work through establishing the most important things that need to happen that week through the weekly Brain Trust Meeting.

# Chapter 16: The End Game

*"Discipline is the bridge between goals and accomplishment."* Jim Rohn

In the week leading up to the birth of Ffion, our first child, we found out that she was pointing in the wrong direction. She was what is known as a breach baby, which can lead to many more problems and risks at birth, both for baby and Mum. As a result, Caryl ended up having an emergency C-Section. Not something we had planned for, and a more clinical and worrying entrance into the world for our first born. The main thing, of course, is that both Caryl and Ffion emerged from it safely.

What that meant though was that, when it came to the birth of our second child, much of the childbirth experience was still new to us. We went through the stages at home with the tens machine providing little to no pain relief. We had the drive into hospital, worrying that we were going too soon, but also worrying that we had left it too late.

The birth didn't go according to plan, and whilst I will spare you the details, it was more drawn out than it should have been. To steal a popular phrase amongst the partners of those giving birth, 'it was like watching your favourite pub burn down!' After a long, drawn-out birth, I started to feel a little queasy.

I've never been great with blood and gore, which is ridiculous as a farmer's son. I can still vividly remember the humiliation of going green in an A-Level biology lesson where we had had to prick our finger with a pin to extract a drop of blood to analyse on under the microscope. What made matters worse was the fact that we had to head through to a second classroom to view the results on a TV screen. There was me, in front of not just one classroom of children but two, told to sat on the floor for fear of me collapsing. All over a single droplet of my own blood.

Anyway, back to the birth of our second child. As a result of feeling queasy, I took a seat next to Caryl, so when our second born did finally arrived, I saw baby's entrance into the world through the arch of Caryl's legs. I have to admit that the next few minutes remain a little blurry as to the exact proceedings, but I definitely remember passing up the opportunity to cut the ambilocal chord; that would have been the straw that broke the camel's back. Then I remember the midwife asking me to tell Caryl whether we had a boy or a girl. Of this I was certain, I had seen the evidence.

We have a boy, a beautiful baby boy, I proclaimed. Having come armed with names to suit both sexes, we announced him to the world as Euan, and he was wrapped up and passed to Caryl for her first cuddle. How perfect, a little baby brother for Ffion. The next steps were obvious. I called my parents and told them of the exciting news. Brenda, Caryl's mum was with us at the time, so I phoned Russell, her father to again share the wonderful news.

After about 20 minutes, the mid wife came back into the room, and asked if she could weigh baby Euan.

"What a lovely name" she remarked, as she up wrapped him to put him onto the scales.

At which point, she let out a small scream. What had happened, what was wrong? As a new parent it is moments like this that seem to last a lifetime. Was there a problem with his breathing? Had she somehow hurt him, or could something else, even more worrying, be wrong? These thoughts flash through your mind at 100 mph.

"I am afraid," she said, "that you do not have a baby boy at all. You do in fact have a beautiful baby girl."

What? How? But I saw…. Clearly after 15 years the memories have faded a little, but I remember being 100% sure of what I had seen. Obviously, I knew that there would be an ambilocal cord, after all I had done A-level biology! I know what I saw, and it was the evidence required to sign off our new baby as a boy. And yet, what I saw, didn't actually exist. It was never there.

Fortunately, Bronwyn, as she was named after a fleeting 20-minute spell as Euan, was born early in the morning. As a result, I got straight back on the phone to my mum and father-in-law to correct my small, but life-defining error.

Thank goodness Bronwyn was born early in the morning, as otherwise it would have probably taken about 3 hours to get through to Mum on the phone, by which time most of the East Midlands would have known we had been blessed with a baby boy, and she may have already submitted the congratulatory notice to the local paper.

The important point is that our eyes do deceive us. I was sure of what I saw, and yet it wasn't ever there. It was my brain, eyes or something playing tricks on me. It is very easy for this to happen in your business. We think something is going well, as from the outside it appears that way. It is only through closer inspection that we can identify where our initial instincts and judgements are floored.

I hope that this book helps you see some of the areas that you can improve in the way that you approach your business, and minimise tiny, but crucial mistakes. However, there is one final piece of the jigsaw is to really clearly know where you are heading: What is the End Game?

We have started to think about this more with the goals that we created as part of The Limitless Life Planner, which can download here and watch the explanation video: **www.thetrusted.team/llp** . If you haven't done this already, it is so important you complete this now. This gives you some clear areas to aim towards. Try and make these as SMART as you can, i.e. Specific, Measurable, Attainable, Relevant and Timely. These should continue to evolve with you though. The more you think about them, the more you can refine them. It is sometimes difficult to clearly think about what you want to be, because it is so difficult to think about life 10 years from now.

In my first few days at Newcastle University, I was introduced to Rob, another 'Agric' (Agriculture student). Like me, Rob was not a typical farmers son, and not a typical 'Agric'. He didn't wear cords and check shirts, but instead, growing up in Cornwall, had more of a lean towards baggy surfer trousers and skater shoes. Instead of wanting to drink beer through a sheep's oesophagus, as the 'Agrics' were renowned for, he'd rather head off to a DJ set to dance the night away. Whilst that wasn't me initially, spending more time hanging out with him, it soon became me.

As much as he rubbed off on me, I did him. He hated football when he arrived in Newcastle; but a combination of my enthusiasm for it, Euro '96 'coming to the Toon' and the infectious Geordie devotion to their team, The Magpies, I soon had him turning into a massive England and Newcastle fan.

Rob was an incredible guy. As quick as he was to take the micky out of his friends, he was also always on hand to help them, and to have a laugh in the process. Whilst he wasn't a typical farmer, unlike me he had a massive passion for farming. He loved his dairy herd and would spend nearly as much time at Uni finding cattle to buy for the herd at home as he would leading me astray. He loved his cows so much that, when I had my 21st birthday party back at our farm in Rutland, instead of showing up with a girlfriend, he arrived with a cow in a trailer that needed a stable for the night.

After Uni, he headed back to the farm in Cornwall, where he started to expand the herd. After Uni, whilst I was travelling, he decided he wanted to join me for a while. We had an amazing couple of months travelling Thailand and Malaysia, doing full moon parties, learning to dive and trekking through Chang Mai together, something that inspired him to go on to travel more too.

I was his best man when he married Sam, a girl at Uni who I had introduced him to. Sadly, that marriage didn't last, but he maintained his love for the farming. He started to expand the farm, diversifying into producing yoghurt drinks, a veal unit with his sister, and anaerobic digestion unit with his brother. I have no doubt that the former of these would now be a household name had what happened next not come to pass.

Whilst his failed marriage to Sam had hit him hard, he got back on track, and Rob was settling down with a new girlfriend and her daughter. Sarah shared his passion for the farm, and Rob was starting to blossom again. On a research trip to Scandinavia with his dad and brother, his divorce from Sam finally came through, and he confessed to his brother that upon his return he would propose to Sarah. Life was starting to take shape again for this incredible guy.

The very next day, Rob and a pilot took at plane for a tour of anaerobic digestion plant they had travelled to see for research. As his brother and dad watched on, then plane nosedived into the ground upon landing. Rob and the pilot were killed instantly.

The news reached me through one of Rob's Cornish friends who I had met when organising his stag do. Obviously, we were all shocked beyond belief. He was 30 years old. He had made such a huge impression on so many people during that relatively short time.

I was honoured to be asked to say a eulogy at his funeral. Probably the toughest public speaking I'll ever do. As we walked out of the church that day, with the sound of Fat Les' football anthem 'Vindaloo' playing in the aisles, I had a thought: This could just as easily be my funeral. I have been on such a similar journey to Rob, why was it him and not me, or someone else? Then I thought, what would this day look like had it been me? What would people think of the 30 years I have spent on this planet? What have I achieved at this point? Would they be proud?

Suddenly, it made me think about my life differently. None of us know how long we will be on this planet, so we have got to get on and live the life we want. This isn't a practice run, we've got to grab life by the proverbials and get on and live the best life we can. There are no second chances.

Take a few minutes to visualise your last hours on Earth and of your funeral. See the people you care most about sitting by your bedside for your last moments. Those same people and more will be attending your funeral, and will be at the wake afterwards.

By looking at the end of your life, I hope it highlights the blessings that surround you today. It should also help you evaluate your life thus far and consider whether you have done the things you want to be remembered for. After imagining the end of your life, you're less likely to think, 'I should have spent a few more hours in the office or replied to my emails a little more promptly'.

Next, take a few minutes to think about what your company could look like 10 years from now. Imagine your company is 10 x bigger than it is today, or maybe 100 x bigger. Think big. What would it look like? We use 'The End Game Enlightenment' at The Trusted Team to achieve this, which takes the process to a whole new level and helps you think even bigger and more creatively.

These are a couple of exercises that maybe could help you to create the best life you can that I do in my Better Future Framework. You can find out more about this at **www.thetrusted.team/bff**.

## Mitigate Risk
*"It's only when the tide goes out that you discover who's been swimming naked."* Warren Buffet

Part of planning the end game is also planning for the worst. It is all very well having this great plan for the future, but one thing is for sure, unexpected things are going to happen along the way that are going to mess this up. It may be big things, and it may be little things, but technologies will disrupt markets, people will quit, fall ill or worse, and fashions will change. As a result, if you want to give yourself the best chance possible of achieving a result, you've got to look at how much risk is involved.

In looking at business opportunities, I look at whether there is a 3:1 risk. I believe that if there is not 3 times the upside to the downside, then it isn't worth doing. Ultimately, none of us know whether something will be a success or not, but if you keep trying things, some will come off and some will inevitably fail. If you have 3 times as much upside to downside, the ones that work, which hopefully will be most, will reward you sufficiently well to make you some money, and to offset the ones that don't.

The same applies to when you are investing your money. You need to see that over the long term the investment returns are likely to be sufficient to offset the risks. Too many people take too much risk with their money when it comes to investing. What they don't realise is that often they take unnecessary risks. Investing successfully, as I said earlier in Chapter 7, is about getting the best growth possible for a level of risk you understand and are comfortable with. It is about protecting yourself in the hard times and benefiting from the growth in the good times. Diversification, thus risk mitigation, allows you to keep your plans on track.

Risks are both good and bad, and if we consider them further and give negativity a role, we can be more powerful.

It might sound counterintuitive, especially in a world that often preaches positivity, but giving negativity a role in your life can be incredibly empowering. Understanding that within every difficulty lies a potential opportunity allows us to engage our problem-solving skills more effectively and creatively. Just like in personal development, where we turn inward to discover our true potential, this tool encourages us to look closely at our challenges and find hidden gems of opportunity.

Take Sylvester Stallone's journey with the original 'Rocky'. Stallone faced immense rejection and was at a point where he had to sell his beloved dog to make ends meet. Despite lucrative offers for his screenplay, he held out to star in the film himself, believing deeply in his vision. His perseverance not only paid off, but it also fundamentally changed his life and career. This story is a powerful reminder that the path to achieving our goals is often littered with obstacles that require us to stand firm and be true to our visions.

Muhammad Ali and Steve Jobs provide other excellent examples of how mindset and perspective can turn obstacles into opportunities. Ali's famous practice of pushing past his limits, and Jobs's ability to create a 'reality distortion field', illustrate how redefining the boundaries of what's possible can lead to extraordinary outcomes.

At The Trusted Team we use a tool called 'The Obstacle Opportunity' that breaks down a large goal into smaller, manageable parts. This is a technique used by triathletes and entrepreneurs alike to maintain focus and drive. For example, dividing an Ironman race into segments allows athletes to manage their energy and maintain a strong pace throughout. Similarly, in business and personal growth, chunking down goals helps maintain momentum and ensures continuous progress, even when the end goal seems distant.

Remember, the journey to achieving our goals is not meant to be easy. It's filled with challenges that test our resolve, creativity, and endurance. But with the right tools, like The Obstacle Opportunity tool, you can transform these challenges into powerful catalysts for growth and success.

I encourage you to adopt this tool in your daily life. Whether you're navigating personal hurdles or professional setbacks, remember that you have the power to turn every obstacle into an opportunity. It's not just about overcoming what's in your path, but also about transforming these challenges into triumphs. Let's harness this tool and make our ambitions a reality, one obstacle at a time!

If you'd like a copy of the tool, please email **hello@thetrusted.team**

## Merge Fun with Business

No one said work cannot be fun. In fact, we should be doing everything possible to make sure that work is as much fun as possible. As you've worked out, I love to swim, cycle and run. I also love to Scuba dive and play golf. In fact, anything that can include all of those activities would rank pretty highly on my list.

I few years ago, I was lucky enough to be able to attend a conference for the top Financial Planners from around the world that was held in Los Angeles. Given the time difference and the fact that I'd never been to LA before, I wanted a day either side of the event to acclimatise and to take a look around. I'd heard loads about it, but never been before.

Having just been on cycling tour in Spain with old school friends, I had a thought: What better opportunity to see the area than to hire a bike and explore, whilst picking off some of my training for my next triathlon? So, I did just that.

Finding a decent bike to rent was a challenge enough, but then trying to identify where to cycle was essentially a dice roll. I read up online, looked at Strava routes, asked friends who had been and contacted the local cycle shops for some recommendations. Eventually I settled on Palos Verdes for an 80-mile circuit before the conference, and Malibu including Mulholland Drive for a 100-mile route afterwards. Both looked and sounded like stunning rides, but I was heading into a completely unknown world.

After collecting my bike, I headed out towards Palos Verdes, the most expensive real estate in LA. I got chatting to a local at some lights and ended up cycling with him for the first 20 or so miles. It turned out he was also a Financial Planner of sorts, so, combined with his cycling trips to Europe, we had loads to chat about whilst we cycled the streets and coastline of LA. He gave me top tips of where to buy coffee and lunch in Palos Verdes, and my ride out was perfect. I took in stunning cliff top views over the Atlantic whilst cycling past incredible but surprisingly understated houses- not at all what I expected from LA. I saw volleyball on Redondo, muscles on Venice Beach and even dolphins on Manhattan Beach. It was a brilliant day's cycling, combined with a delicious seafood lunch overlooking the Atlantic Ocean.

However, the day cycling in Malibu wasn't quite as successful. I realised over the course of my stay in LA that cycling from Santa Monica along the Pacific Coast Highway was going to be risky business. For the first 20+ miles of my route, I feared for my life as I dodged gas-guzzling juggernauts, so decided to swap my bike for a ride in a friendly Uber taxi.

Once in Malibu I jumped back on the bike and headed up into the hills and canyons. It was hot, unsurprisingly, and what remained of my route was nothing but climbing and descending. The views were stunning, the cycling some of the best I've done, and the conditions perfect, but again things didn't go according to plan.

I discovered that my planned pit stop only opens on the weekend, so I had no chance to refuel or fill the water bottle. My next option of a stop amazingly didn't have a shop, garage or even an ice cream van anywhere to be seen. Twice over the course of my route I had to wonder into a random vineyard and whilst they didn't have food to buy that was any use to me, they kindly allowed me to refill my water bottles. After all, with all this climbing and hot sun, I was getting through a lot of it! Instead of my wonderful 100-mile day of cycling through the mansions of Malibu, I ended up with a somewhat stressed and hungry.

And that's just the cycling! I ran some interesting routes around LA on the mornings of my conference; never really knowing whether the gangland LA I heard about in rap music was around the next corner. I didn't brave a sea swim, as I just couldn't find the research to tell me it was safe, and the hotel pool proved to only be open while I was in the conference.

So, why was my first day of cycling so much better than my second? I think it was partly down to the fact that I met that local. The conversation, his local knowledge, and the companionship was the difference between my successful Palos Verdes cycling versus my unsuccessful Malibu adventure, and that got me thinking: Wouldn't it have been amazing if I could have easily found a group of local cyclists who were around the same pace as me and who were heading out around the time I was? I know if the shoe was on the other foot that I would love to act as tour guide for the day to a traveller staying in my part of the world. Joining up with a local group of keen peddlers could have made my LA cycling even more special and avoided me making my Malibu mistakes.

In addition to my cycling, perhaps I could have also run with a local running group, who'd have taken me on the best and safest routes the city had to offer. Perhaps an open water swimming group could have given me the confidence to explore the LA waters too.

But every cloud has a silver lining. This trip inspired me to create a new podcast called 'Tribeathlon', which is now called 'The Business of Endurance'. The podcast features guest speakers from the world of endurance sport, and takes the lessons they have learnt and applies these to your business and life. If you're into sport and a business owner, take a look. I love producing it, so hope you love listening too.

We have amazing guests from the world of triathlon, such as Mark Allen, world-class runners such as Eilish McColgan and Damian Hall, and adventure sports people like Mark

Beaumont and Sean Conway. It's an exciting and inspiring mix!

Over the years I have found fellow cyclists, runners and swimmers to be some of the friendliest people I know. It seems to go with the territory. Miles are our meditation, and that seems to make us nice people.

The Business of Endurance has been a way of me making more of my work life about the things I love. In time I plan for it to mean I spend more time in that world. I am trying to merge my fun with my business life, because no one said work can't be fun.

The other silver lining I found by going to the global conference in LA, was that I not only got learn how I can improve my business, but I got to cycle and run my way around an incredible part of the world for the first time. I now attend most years and have been fortunate enough to be able to also speak at it, sharing some of the ideas in this book with 12,500 of the top Financial Advisers from around the world. Whenever I'm there, whether it's in Miami, LA, Boston, or another part of the world, I also plan my free days, where I head out to see the sights and make new memories, a lot of the time on my bike.

This may sound like a holiday, but for me it isn't. Whilst cycling for roughly 16 hours, I will be listening to business books, and coming up with ways to improve our business over the next year. Whilst travelling to and from an excursion, whilst flying, or whilst running, I'll be doing exactly the same. I see this time as an amazing opportunity to brainstorm ideas of how I can take my businesses to the next level. Not just from the top speakers and spending time with my peers, but through a total immersion in learning whilst I am away. In fact, this is actually what Bill Gates and Steve Jobs, to name but a few, were doing at the peak of their careers. Taking a week out of their business to travel to somewhere that allowed them to read, think and set up the next set of goals for their business. It didn't serve them too badly now did it.

What I have realised over time is that my primary role in our businesses is to think, and to come up with ideas for others to implement. The wonderful thing about that is that thinking can be done anywhere. It can be done in different parts of the world, whilst doing different activities, and can be stimulated in different ways. That means there is more opportunity to merge fun with work.

Finally, I know that the golf club is a great place to meet new clients. I don't actively go looking for them, but over the course of a 4-hour round of golf, you cannot help but talk about what you do; and that leads to opportunities. So, leaving early one day a week to play golf not only makes business sense, I enjoy it.

How can you merge what you do for a living with what you enjoy? As the business owner, you can engineer this, if you put your mind to it. Turn your business life into your leisure life, and you'll never work a day again! This may sound selfish, but as an entrepreneur you should be a little selfish.

Create a business that not only delivers the most value to your clients, the most opportunity to grow for your team, but also the life that you want to live. This is your life, you only get one as far as I am aware, so make sure you spend it doing the things you want.

It will come as no surprise that we have a tool for this concept too! It's called 'The Fun Fusion Formula' and it helps to inject passion, opportunities, and, obviously, fun, into your business and life.

## Have a Plan and Stick to It

As I have already mentioned earlier in the book, I seem to be perpetually training for my next Ironman! 2.4 miles of swimming, 112 miles of cycling, and then the small issue of a 26.2 mile run to finish. I have lost count of the number of people who question how I can have the time to do the training required for these events, run a business and have time to see my family. It is all about planning, and, as may have gathered, that is what this book is all about.

About 6 years ago, I ran my first marathon in Brighton with 3 of the Efficient Portfolio team. Whilst this wasn't a brilliant idea for the training I needed for my first ever Ironman training, as the recovery is too long and risk of injury too high, I needed to have done it for the confidence. Imagine swimming and cycling for around 7 hours, and then embarking on your longest ever run. I needed to mentally have banked a marathon, so I knew I could do it again.

When chatting to a couple of the guys I swim with over a coffee one morning, then mentioned about the run/walk/run strategy created by Jeff Galloway. Like with most things, I went off and did some more research. Then I tried it, and it seemed to help me run further, with less pain both during and afterwards. This may sound like a strategy only used by the very slowest runners, but in my research I found someone called Mitch Phillips that had run a sub-3-hour marathon with this approach. That was never going to be me, but I had mentally targeted sub-4-hours, so this seemed like a helpful approach to try.

As a result, for my training and for the marathon itself, I did a 9-minute run to 1-minute walk strategy, right from the start. This worked well, with the exception of the first couple of walking sections. The mental torment of walking just 9 minutes into the marathon, with the crowd shouting things like "come on mate, you can do it" was more difficult than I had anticipated. I just had to stare down at my watch to ignore them, in the hope that they realised it was part of the strategy.

However, what it allowed me to do was to stick to 9-minute miles throughout, which I knew would get me in under 4 hours. I finished in 3.57, which I was really pleased with. The last few miles up hill into a headwind were tough, but I managed to maintain the same pace. The beauty of the run/walk/run strategy was that whilst everyone around me was slowing down, I was maintaining the same pace. I was also thinking, if this hurts now, imagine how is it going to feel having cycled 112 miles and swam 2.4 miles prior to starting, which is what the Ironman would bring!

Experience now tells me that this is a fantastic strategy. It's one of the steps I take to succeeding in my sporting endeavours.

Dan Sullivan of The Strategic Coach® Program talks about the four steps he's observed to create breakthrough results in business. He calls it 'The 4 C's Formula®[2]':

---

[2] Source: **www.StrategicCoach.com**

**Commitment**. First, you have to take a leap of faith and really commit to what you want to achieve—commit before you have crossed every 't' and dotted every 'I'. There's no doubt that this is scary.

**Courage**. Most people admire courage in others but don't like the experience themselves. In fact, this crucial step feels awful. You've committed yourself without having any proof that what you're going after is going to pay off.

**Capability**. Think back to one of your breakthroughs. Wasn't it the combination of making a commitment and going through a period requiring a lot of courage that created both the new capability and the new confidence?

**Confidence**. The new level of confidence you experience after a breakthrough is what gives you the ability to commit to an even bigger breakthrough and an even greater sense of confidence. And the process repeats itself.

By setting the goal to run a marathon, it was a leap of faith. Following making the commitment, I began to build up the courage to actually go and do it. I then started to research things like the Run/Walk/Run strategy, so that I had the capability. That meant, on the day, I had the confidence to carry out the plan.

This is why The Limitless Life Planner works so well. It is forcing you to make and revisit your commitments for a better future. As time passes you gain the courage, but you also start to find the resources that are going to give you the capability.

This is what allowed me to write my first book. Initially setting the commitment as a goal on The Limitless Life

Planner, I had no idea what the book would be about; I just knew I wanted to write a book. Over time, I found the courage to narrow down my subject and I end up selecting the subject of retirement planning.

As I did more research on the subject I realised that retirement wasn't just about the money. It was about how people spent their time in retirement, and how they kept themselves fit, healthy and happy. I developed the capabilities to write about each of these areas. That gave me the confidence to get 'The Dream Retirement: How to Secure Your Money and Retire Happy' published in 2015. You can download a free copy of the book at **www.thetrusted.team/books/the-dream-retirement** if you wish.

The same applies to the 1 Page Business Plan. You are making the commitments for your business. As Dan Sullivan says, 'Commitment ultimately leads to the Confidence to achieve it'.

If you'd like to see a live demonstration of The 1 Page Business Plan, the best place is during my Limitless Life Workshop, which can be found here: **www.thetrusted.team/the-limitless-life-workshop**

## Monday Morning Routine
*"Own your morning. Elevate your life."* Robin Sharma

The key to achieving your goals is to have a great system, and to revisit it regularly. As I said earlier, 'losers have goals, winners have systems'. The best way to do this is to build it into you're the Happy Week. Build it into your schedule so that it happens, without fail, every week. For me, this is best done on a Monday morning, but that doesn't have to be the same for you. Monday, as you now know, is my 'Team Focus' day, ensuring they are all organised to achieve what we need to do that week. It is also the start of the week, when you are perhaps most likely to feel demotivated about being back in the office. As a result, it is a great time to set up an amazing week, as this will energise you for the week ahead.

Here is my Monday Morning routine:

1. 1-hour Swim: A great way to energise yourself for the day ahead and clear out any cobwebs.

Once in the office I then complete the following, in this order:

1. **Achievements**: Essentially a quick version of The Best Things Exercise, I always start with a positive. I list the best personal and best business things that have happened in the last week. I do this on my Limitless Life Planner.

2. **Diary Review**: Look at the week ahead to remind yourself what is happening when, so that you can identify the best times to do specific tasks, because we need to ensure we are only doing 'Focus Activities' on 'Focus Days' where possible.

3. **Goal Review:** Read that month's Limitless Life Planner goals. I'll also add anything relevant to these goals that needs to be done that week into my capture list. In addition, on the first Monday of each month, and also the first week of each quarter, I will

write my new Monthly/Quarterly Goals to my Capture List.

4. **Capture List:** By building my capture list on The Limitless Life Planner, I have a list of things to do next week or month, so I'll review those and add them to my capture list. I'll also look at the week ahead and identify any other to do items and add them. This is your opportunity to get down any thoughts that have been banging around in your head. Don't do them now, just add them to the capture list.

5. **Ideas on the Move:** From the notes on my phone I take any ideas that I have had during that week and either add them to my capture list, or to The Team Planner, to discuss at The Brain Trust Meeting.

6. **Successful Business Scorecard:** I'll review this document in detail, so I know what is happening in our business. Anything I spot that needs attention will go on The Team Planner to discuss at The Brain Trust Meeting.

7. **Time System Split:** As I talked about in Chapter 12, I split my time into Free, Focus and Buffer days. In order to ensure I am constantly improving my balance in these areas, I record how many I have that week. That way at the end of the year I can see what percentage of my time focused on each of these.

8. **Crucial Results:** As a result of reading my goals for the month, I ask myself what the most important things are I need to do this week to allow me to hit my goals. This ensures I am constantly moving towards my monthly, quarterly, yearly, and therefore my lifetime goals, every single week.

9. **Training Plan:** In order to ensure I complete the required fitness training for that week, I ensure that every element of it is diarised. Typically, I have done this before I get to Monday morning, but this is my final opportunity to ensure the time I need for swimming, running and cycling is planned.

10. **Allocate the Capture list:** Go through the Capture List of jobs for the week ahead and allocate them to specific days. Group complimentary activities together, so that you can work more effectively. With every task think, 'could I delegate this to someone else in my team? If so, how can I ensure I always delegate this going forward?' If you can, move it to The Team Planner so that you have the follow up to make sure it gets done.

If you adopt and then adapt this approach to your life, you will be astonished at how much you can achieve. When you look back a few years from now at the goals that you are setting today, what seem like huge asks will more than likely have become easily realised achievements.

## Making It Happen
*"The only way to fail is to not try."* Charlie Reading

That last point is so important. It is very easy to get caught up in what you didn't do. If you have a goal to get to the stars and you fall short, you may hit the moon. By setting massive goals, whether you hit them all or not is not the important thing: It is about achieving so much more than you would have done otherwise. When you look back, you can beat yourself up for missing the bits you didn't do, or you can celebrate the success of what you did.

When I wrote the first version of this book, we had grown our new business levels by 50% in 5 of the last 6 years. In 2018, for quarter 1, 2 and 3 we were on track to do the same again. Then a combination of Brexit and falling markets led to an unusually quiet quarter 4. As a result, we missed out 50% target. We still grew our new business by over 30%, but we missed our target. I could have been down about missing that target, but I wasn't. I celebrated the success of growing by over 30%, which by many companies' standards is still amazing. And we celebrated that success as a team.

Around that time, my very talented wife, Caryl, had her first art exhibition. It was a wonderful evening showing off her amazing work to friends, clients and family at Portfolian House. The exhibition was comprised of art that Caryl had taken over 2 years to produce and it was an incredible journey of discovery for her.

Over the course of the evening, chatting to friends over a glass or two of fizz, in addition to raving about Caryl's art, several people commented on how well our business was doing. Liz Moore, a good friend of ours and very talented chef who caters for our events, happened to pass comment on how happy the entire Efficient Portfolio team always seemed to be. Other friends commented on never having time to do the exercise they want, let alone find the time to train for an Ironman. Others told me about how lucky I was to be able to go cycling and diving all as part of my working life.

I am not telling you this to impress you. I am telling you this to impress upon you that everything I have talked about in this book has had a tremendous impact on both my life and my business. This is from a dyslexic lad who struggled at school and generally lacked motivation for most things. I am not saying I have achieved the perfect balance by any means. I am not saying I am making as much money as I would like to, as there is always scope to improve. I am not saying my businesses run perfectly, or that I absolutely love every minute of my working day.

Life is not a game of perfect. What I am doing, however, is appreciating the success that a determination to create the best business and life possible has brought me so far. Clearly there is always scope for everything to be better, but I am practicing what I preach, and celebrating the 80% success rather than waiting for the 100% that will never come.

Within this book are the secrets to my success so far. The exercises contain all the magic, because it isn't the principles I teach that will ultimately deliver the results, but rather the questions I ask. I encourage you to go to **www.thetrusted.team/books/entrepreneurial-happiness** to download the workbook and complete the exercises if you haven't done them already.

If you have, congratulations on taking a massive step towards a better future, both financially and personally. If you want to take this a step further, you can by becoming part of my Trusted Team where I will guide you on how you can create more entrepreneurial happiness in your life. You can find out more about this at **www.thetrusted.team/packages**.

I also occasionally do some 1-to-1 coaching for business owners, so if that is something that interests you, please drop me a line at **charlie@thetrusted.team** . If you are young, and just starting your own business for the first time, also drop me a line as I am even more occasionally willing to do some free coaching, as I love helping young people at the start of their journey.

Complete in full The Limitless Life Planner, watch our free virtual workshops and book your coaching call. These, in conjunction with using the Monday Morning Routine, allow it to evolve every week into what will become your life's work. Utilise The Team Planner to ensure you get the best out of your team and you successfully delegate more. Diarise your Quarterly Leadership Meetings, your weekly Brain Trust meetings and your monthly Kaizen Meetings, because this will ensure everyone knows where they are going, what you are all doing and how it is getting done over a train frame that keeps you accountable. Build your Successful Business Scorecard so you can keep track of your business and identify any future problems as early as possible.

Finally, accept that life is not a game of perfect. Doing all of these things at 80% is far better than trying to get any one area to 100%. Procrastination is a fear of starting;

perfectionism is a fear of finishing. Just accept that nothing will ever be perfect, and you will get a whole lot more done. It will allow you to market more, it will allow you to delegate more, and finally, it will allow you to be healthier and happier.

It has been an absolute pleasure sharing with you so many of the amazing discoveries I have made over the years. I hope you can use them to create a better life and business for yourself as I have done with them. I am blessed to be surrounded by a family that I love, a team that I am inspired by and clients who genuinely value what we do for them.

If you would like to know more about what we are up to, how you can create a better financial future or where you can attend one of our events, you can find out more at **www.thetrusted.team**.

Remember, if you make the same decisions today as you made yesterday, you'll get the same results tomorrow as you got today. If you go ahead and make some significant decisions, that will lead to significant changes in your life, and you too will reach entrepreneurial happiness!

## Chapter Summary

- This life is not a practice run. You need to step up and create the life you want now; not at some point in the future. You don't know when your time will be up!
- Protect your future plans through identifying key risks to you, your family and your business, so that when the unexpected happens, it doesn't derail the plan.

- Work doesn't have to be a chore. Work can be fun. Identify ways that you can merge work with the activities you enjoy, and to coin a phrase, "You'll never work a day in your life!"
- Achieve more in your life by building a plan and executing it.
- Achieve more in less time by having an amazing Monday Morning Routine to allow you to delegate, delete or do the most impactful items on your to do list.

Printed in Great Britain
by Amazon